CORFU

A complete traveller's guide, with 180 colour photographs, which takes
visitors on a tour of Corfu and informs them about the island's
archaeological sites, museums, sights, arts and history.

EDITING & DTP: BARRAGE LTD
TEXTS: MARIA MAVROMATAKI (archaeologist, tour guide)
ENGLISH TRANSLATION: COX & SOLMAN
ART EDITING: FOTINI SVARNA

PHOTOGRAPHS: HAÏTALIS PUBLISHING Co. ARCHIVE

PUBLICATIONS HAITALIS
13 ASTROUS STR., 13121 ATHENS
TEL.: 5766.883

CORFU

CONTENTS

POSITION - GEOGRAPHY - ECONOMY

pp. 6-7

Corfu, richly endowed by nature and history, has a landscape full of variety and a wealth of images and colours to offer its visitors.

Facing page: Rock formations at Sidari

C orfu is the most northerly of the large islands of the Ionian Sea, and is second only to Cephalonia, among those islands, in terms of area. With Cephalonia, Zakynthos, Lefkada, Paxoi, Ithaki and Kythera it forms the administrative group known as the Ionian Islands. The Prefecture of Corfu consists of Corfu itself, Paxoi, Antipaxoi, Othoni, Ereikousa and Mathraki. The island lies at the mouth of the Adriatic Sea, close to the mainland coast of Greece and Albania, from which it became geographically separated in the distant past. Cape Ayios Stefanos, in the northern part of the island, is only 2.5 km. from the mainland of Albania. Corfu has an area of 592 sq. km. and a population of 92,000.

The island is elongated and sickle-shaped. In the north, the maximum width from east to west is 21 km., gradually dwindling as we move south until the island is only 7 km. wide at its southernmost extremity. The coastline of Corfu is widely varied. In the east, the land slopes gently down to charming little bays and coves. The largest bays on the east side are those of Corfu town and Lefkimmi, while on the west, where the coastline is steep and rocky, there are tiny inlets, many of them of the greatest beauty. All around Corfu are islets, including Vido and Lazareto in the bay of Corfu town, and the famous Pontikonisi close to the Chalkiopoulou lagoon.

Most of the ground on Corfu is low-

p. 8
In most places, the coastline of Corfu slopes gently down to attractive little bays.

Above: cove at Benitses.

Below: view of Sidari.

lying, though there are three ranges of moderately high hills. The highest peak, Mt Pantokratoras (906 m.), is in the north-east of the island, with the peaks of Vistonas and Araklis further to the west. A lower range whose highest peak is Mt Ayii Deka (576 m.) runs cross-wise across the centre of the island, with the Ropa valley further to the north and the low hills of Chlomos (330 m.) in a southerly direction. Close to this is Lake Korission, with a length of 12 km. and a maximum width of 1,300 m., separated from the sea by a narrow spit of sand. There are few rivers, almost all of which run dry during the summer. The largest of them is the Mesongi river, which rises on Mt Ayii Deka and flows into the sea in the bay of Corfu town.

The climate of Corfu is of the category known as maritime Mediterranean, with cool summers (when the temperature averages 27°C) and mild winters (average temperature 10°C). In

Greek terms, the humidity is relatively high, thanks to the prevailing north-westerly and westerly winds, which cause abundant rainfall throughout the year. As a result, the island is thickly wooded and its landscape is idyllically verdant. The soil is extremely fertile, particularly favouring the cultivation of olives, grapes, citrus fruit, cereals and vegetables. The incomparable natural beauty of Corfu and the vast variety of crops that could be grown there made the island famous even in ancient times. Homer refers admiringly to "fruitful" Corfu in the following words: "*Without the court and close beside its gate is a large garden, covering four acres; around it runs a hedge on either side. Here grow tall thrifty trees - pears, pomegranates, apples with shining fruit, sweet figs and thrifty olive. On them fruit never fails; it is not gone in winter or in summer, but lasts throughout the year; for constantly the west wind's breath brings some to bud and mellows*

p. 9

Palaiokastritsa, standing above the six bays on the deeply indented coastline, is one of the prettiest places on the island.

p. 10

Since antiquity, the olive tree has been among the island's most important resources.

Above: Scene from the olive harvest.

Below: Mountain landscape.

others. Pear ripens upon pear, apple on apple, cluster on cluster, fig on fig. Here too the teeming vineyard has been planted, one part of which, the drying place, lying on level ground, is heating in the sun; elsewhere men gather grapes; and elsewhere still they tread them."

The basic feature of the landscape of Corfu is, of course, its vast forests of olive trees, which are also a most important source of income for the local people. Our first information about the cultivation of olives on the island dates as far back as the Mycenean period, and comes from archaeological evidence and from the texts of Homer. However, it

would seem that the vine was the most important crop in the agricultural economy for many centuries after this time, and that the olive had been neglected until the arrival of the Venetians in the fourteenth century. In 1386, the Venetians resolved to try to monopolise the olive oil market and to compete with the Genoese, and so they implemented a policy of large-scale planting with olive trees. Special decrees provided economic incentives for the cultivation of olives, and sanctions were even taken against those who refused to replace their existing crops with olives. By 1766, as many as 1,900,000 olive trees had been

p. 11

The soil of Corfu is unusually fertile, and the islanders grow a wide variety of crops in and around their verdant villages.

planted on Corfu, most of them on soil which had not previously been cultivated because it was not suitable for other crops. Today, the number of olive trees on Corfu has reached 3,500,000, and they belong to a special variety in which the tree grows unusually tall. The fruit of these trees is small, and the oil produced from it is of exceptionally high quality. The olive harvest in Corfu lasts some six months - unlike the rest of Greece, where one month or at most two is needed; this is because on Corfu the fruit is allowed to drop from the branches as it ripens and the tree is not beaten, which often results in the fruit being damaged. Although time-consuming, the procedure adopted on Corfu is a guarantee that the olives will be of excellent quality.

Viticulture is now the second most important agricultural activity on Corfu. The lush vineyards, covering some 7% of the total area of arable land, produce grapes suitable for high-quality red and white wine. Corfu is also known as a centre for the production of the rare plant koum kwat, grown only - in Greece - on the island of Chios. The koum kwat tree, imported from Asia, grows to a height of 2.5 - 3.5 m. and its fruit - 2.5 - 3.5 cm. in diameter - resembles tiny oranges. Special processes are used to make a liquer by the same name

pp. 12-13
There is a close bond between the Corfiots and their land with its rich harvests. They feel themselves to be a part of nature, and they are also the direct continuation of Corfiot history and culture.

from the tasty fruit of the tree.

Farming still employs 70% of the work force of the island of Corfu. The other branches of the economy in which large numbers of local people are employed are stock-breeding and fishing. Among the animal products of the island are excellent sausages and salamis, while the delicious lobsters of Palaiokastritsa and Othoni are justly famous. Light and heavy industry make a scant contribution to the economy of the island, which now relies heavily on tourism. Corfu's geographical position, historical past and natural beauties have made it today one of the most impor-

tant resort areas in Greece. Visitors to Corfu will find there a full range of tourist facilities (including luxury hotels and beaches with a wide range of amenities), a good network of roads, a more than adequate public transport system, plenty of scope for numerous sports, frequent cultural and artistic events, and restaurants, bars and discos beyond number. During the summer months, the population of Corfu triples with the influx of visitors, yet there are always quiet corners and serene beaches to be found, and the hospitality of the Corfiots, renowned since ancient times, is inexhaustible.

pp. 14-15
Modern Corfu has excellent tourist facilities and has developed into one of the most cosmopolitan islands in the Mediterranean.

THE MYTHICAL PAST

p. 16-17

Most of our information about the mythical past of Corfu comes from Homer. In this illustration, we see a bust of the great poet of ancient Greece, from the Achilleio on Corfu.

Facing page: The mythical figure of Gorgo, from the pediment of the temple of Artemis.

ccording to tradition, the modern Greek name for the island - Kerkyra - came from the Nymph **Cercyra** (or Corcyra in the Doric dialect), who was the daughter of the river-god Asopus. The god Poseidon fell in love with the beautiful maiden, abducted her, and lay with her on the island. The fruit of their union was Phaeax, the mythical primogenitor of the Phaeaceans who lived on Corfu in antiquity. According to another version of the story, the name of the Nymph Cercyra is cognate with the demonic ancient deity Gorgyra or Gorgo. This view has been reinforced by the discoveries made at a temple of Artemis found near the capital of the island: on the pediment of the temple was a depiction of precisely this demon Gorgo, who may well have been a kind of mythological forerunner to Artemis herself.

Many other names are used for Corfu in the literature of the ancient Greeks. Its length caused it to be called **Makris** (= long), and its shape **Drepane** (= sickle). According to information preserved by Hesiod and Apollonius of Rhodes, the name Drepane was connected with the creation myth involving Cronus and Zeus. When Zeus, with a sickle, cut off the genitals of his father Cronus, the drops of blood gave birth to the Furies, the Nymphs and the Phaeaceans. The sickle itself was stolen by Demeter, who hid it beneath the soil of Corfu, which later - after inundation by the tide - took the shape of the sickle which lay concealed within it.

During the Middle Ages, the name **Corypho**

(from 'coryphi', a peak) came to be used for the twin-peaked acropolis occupied by the Old Fortress of Corfu town, to which the city had been confined after a raid by the Goths in the sixth century AD. This name was the origin of the nomenclature **Corfu**, by which, of course, the island is known today everywhere in the world except Greece.

A still earlier name is given by Homer, in the *Odyssey*: **Scheria**, the famous country of the Phaeaceans. According to the myths, Demeter begged Poseidon to stop (the ancient Greek verb 'schein', hence Scheria) the flow of silt from a river on the mainland so as to prevent it from blocking up the Corfu channel. The name Scheria is associated with the wanderings of Odysseus and his return to his homeland of Ithaca.

Homer tells us that Scheria was inhabited by the Phaeacians, who had originally lived in distant Hyperia. The initiative for the move from Hyperia to Scheria belonged to the mythical King Nausithous, son of Poseidon and Periboea. When Nausithous arrived in Scheria, he *"raised a castle all around the town, built houses, made temples to the gods, and shared out fields" (Odyssey* VII, 9-

10). His sons were called Alcinous and Rexenor, the latter of whom died young, but not before fathering a daughter called Arete. Alcinous married Arete, who was renowned above all other women for her beauty, her virtue and her wisdom. The couple had five sons and a daughter called Nausicaa, and they ruled on Scheria until advanced old age. The narratives of Homer and Apollonius tells us that the royal couple ruled the peace-loving Phaeaceans prudently and justly. Beneath the authority of Alcinous were twelve elders, who headed the assembly of the Phaeacians of which all the islanders were members. When decisions had to be taken, the king convened the assembly and all citizens had the right to speak.

Homer's description of the palace of Alcinous (*Odyssey* VII, 86-136) is unique in its eloquence and power: "*A sheen as of the sun or moon played through the high-roofed houses of generous Alcinous. On either hand ran walls of bronze from threshold to recess, and round about the ceiling was a cornice of dark metal. Doors made of gold closed in the solid building. The doorposts were of silver and stood on a bronze threshold, silver the lintel overhead, and gold the*

pp. 18-19

A view of the Old Fortress in Corfu town. The two rocky peaks on which the castle stands were responsible for giving the town, and later the entire island, its name in the Western languages.

handle. On the two sides were gold and silver dogs; these had Hephaestus wrought with subtle craft to guard the house of generous Alcinous, creatures immortal, young forever".

It was in the time of Alcinous that the famous Odysseus came to the island and received the hospitality of its people. After the Greek victory in the Trojan War, Odysseus had incurred the wrath of Poseidon and for ten long years had wandered stormy seas and inhospitable shores, unable to come to Ithaca, the homeland for which he yearned. When he was washed up on Scheria, he was at death's door after fighting the waves for two whole days and nights. Now the sharp rocks of the island's shore threatened him, but the goddess Athena came to his rescue and helped him come to land on a quiet beach, where Odysseus fell asleep under some trees, with whose leaves he was able to cover his naked body.

When dawn broke, Odysseus heard the happy voices of girls at play and awoke. Nearby were the princess Nausicaa and her friends, playing at ball after washing their clothes in a stream. The beauty of Nausicaa robbed Odysseus of speech for a moment: *"I am your suppliant, princess. Are you some god or mortal? If one of the gods who hold the open sky, to Artemis, daughter of mighty Zeus, in beauty, height and bearing I find you likest [...] For I never before saw such a being with these eyes - no man, no woman. I am amazed to see. At Delos once, by Apollo's altar, something like you I noticed, a young palm-shoot springing up. [...] And just as when I looked on that I marvelled long within, since never before sprang such a stalk from earth; so, lady, I admire and marvel now at you, and greatly fear to touch your knees"* (Odyssey VI, 151-171). And the girl, too, was overcome with admiration for the stranger and rushed to help him, anointing his hair with olive oil to clean it and giving him clothes to wear. After this, Odysseus was fed and invited to the palace. *"Hearken, my white-armed women:* says Nausicaa, *"while I speak. Not without purpose on the part of all the gods that hold Olympus is this man's meeting with the godlike Phaeacians. A while ago he really seemed to me ill-looking, but now he is like the gods who hold the open sky. Ah, might a man like this be called my husband, having his home here, and content to stay! But give, my women, to the stranger food and drink".*

Now Odysseus left the beach where he had come ashore and crossed the city of the Phaeaceans, with *"its tall towers, its fine harbour, the market, the temple of Poseidon and the grove of Athena"*(VII, 264-265). Reaching the palace, he presented himself to Queen Arete. The king willingly offered the hero hospitality, and on the following day summoned the assembly of the Phaeacians in order to take the resolution that they would help the stranger return to his homeland. Athletic contests were held in his honour and a sumptuous banquet was given, during the course of which the bard Demodocus sang of the glory of those who had fought at Troy, causing Odysseus to be deeply moved. In his emotional turmoil, the brave king of Ithaca revealed his identity to Alcinous, telling of his adventures since the fall of Troy. The Phaeacians were thus the first to learn, astonished, of Odysseus' wanderings through the lands of Ciconians, the Lotus-Eaters and the Cyclopes, to the islands of Aeolus and of Circe, to the places where he was beset by the Sirens, by Scylla and Charybdis, and the god Helius, and to the island of Calypso where he had spent so many years. Full of admiration for the hero, the nobles of the island showered him with rich gifts and on the very next day made ready one of their ships to take him safely home to Ithaca.

Since the Phaeacians were descended directly from the sea-god Poseidon, whose son Nausithous had been, it was not surprising that they were known as skilful sailors. *"The Phaeacians care not for bows, but only for masts and oars and long ships, which they gladly speed across the foam"* (*Odyssey* VII, 272-274). However, their decision to give Odysseus one of their ships ran counter to Poseidon's wishes, and they paid dearly for their noble gesture. Poseidon turned their ship to stone as it sailed home from Ithaca and shut off the approaches to their city with a high mountain, thus bringing to pass an oracle received many years before. *"And now Alcinous addressed them thus: 'Ah, surely then the ancient oracles are come to pass, told by my father, who said Poseidon was displeased because we were safe guides for all mankind; and he averred the god one day would wreck a shapely ship of the Phaeacians, returning home from pilgrimage upon the misty sea, and so would throw a lofty mound around our city. That was the old man's tale, and now it all comes true. However, what I say let us all follow: stop piloting the men who come from time to time here to our city; and to Poseidon let us offer twelve choice bulls, that he may have compassion'"* (*Odyssey* XIII, 180-191). This would seem to have been the way in which the islanders interpreted certain rock formations which can still be seen today, close to the coastline of Corfu.

Homer's story about the hospitality of the Phaeacians, who were always glad to receive visitors, is confirmed by the *Argonautica* of the third century BC author Apollonius of Rhodes. According to his account, Odysseus was not the first mythical visitor to Scheria: the Argonauts, led by Jason and ac-

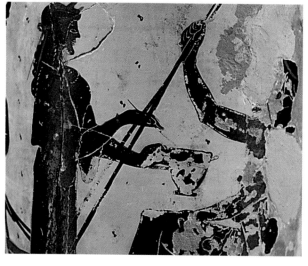

p. 22

The Phaeacians of Corfu were the first people to hear Odysseus' tale of his wanderings after the Trojan War. In this illustration, Odysseus on Circe's island (black-figure lecythus, fifth century BC).

companied by Medea, had preceded them. When Jason fled from Colchis with the Golden Fleece, Medea's father, King Aeëtes, sent a detachment of soldiers in pursuit, and Jason sought refuge in the palace of Alcinous. There, in a cave near what was called the Hyllaean Harbour, he and Medea were married so that the foreign princess would never be able to

return home. But the men of Colchis, whom Alcinous and Arete had also greeted hospitably, refused to sail back to Colchis, where they would have to face the wrath of King Aeëtes, and settled permanently on Scheria.

The actual position of the Homeric city of the Phaeacians has never been found, and no traces of a palace in any way similar to that of

Alcinous have come to light. From time to time, archaeologists have advanced various theories and hypotheses about the Homeric city, which they have identified with Palaiokastritsa and Ermones, but none of them have been confirmed. Hardly any finds from the Mycenean period, to which Homer's narrative refers, have been discovered. Of course, Homer himself lived in the eighth century BC, and his description may have been influenced by what he knew of the Corcyra of his own day. It is thus possible to tentatively identify Homer's Scheria with the site on which a city of the historical period has been discovered; the city visited by Odysseus may lie beneath the ruins of this settlement.

p. 23

Odysseus, lashed to the mast of his ship, listens in enchantment to the sweet song of the Sirens - one of his adventures before he reached the mythical island of Scheria (Roman relief, the Louvre).

THE HISTORICAL PAST

1. ANCIENT HISTORY

T he course of the history of Corfu has been directly connected with its geographical position. As a crossroads between east and west, it has seen the passage of numerous conquerors across its soil. The island seems to have been first inhabited in the Palaeolithic period (30,000 - 7,000 BC), as evidenced by finds which came to light in the Grava cave at Gardiki in the south west of Corfu. These very early inhabitants must have crossed from the coast of Epirus, from which the island had not yet then been separated. The Palaiokastritsa area has yielded finds date from the Late Palaeolithic and Mesolithic periods, and the sites of various Neolithic settlements have been discovered, the most important of which is at Sidari on the north coast (6000 - 2600 BC). The Neolithic civilisation of Corfu, and the Bronze Age culture which followed it (3000 - 1100 BC), have much more in common with the prehistoric cultures of Apulia in southern Italy than they do with the culture of mainland Greece, and there are traces of influence from other parts of the Balkans. Although Homer has left us an extensive description of the Mycenean palace of Alcinous and of the Phaeacian people, giving characteristics which can be placed as belonging to the second millennium BC, very little evidence about the Mycenean inhabitants of the island has so far been found (Ermones, Kefali, Afionas).

We know almost as little about the Illyrians, a people who came from the Dalmatian coast and probably settled in Corfu before the eighth century BC, during the epoch known as the

p. 25

Part of the Doric temple at Kardaki in the Mon Repos estate (late sixth century BC).

Geometric period. The geographer Strabo calls these people Liburnians, and they have now been identified as Illyrians.

The first settlement of Greeks on Corfu of which we can be sure took place around 760-750 BC, and the expedition set out from the city of Eretria in Euboea. This colony was part of a general colonising movement which occurred during the eighth century BC, and the Eretrians were particularly prominent in it as part of

their rivalry with Chalcis, the other strong city of Euboea. During the brief life of the Eretrian colony, Corfu became an important trading post which sent timber for the construction of ships back to the mother city and functioned as a bridge for the further expansion of Eretria into the west.

In 734 BC, the Corinthians - who had now embarked on a programme of colonisation of their own - drove the Eretrians out of Corfu and settled there them-

pp. 26-27
View of Corfu town, with the Old Fortress and Garitsa Bay. In the background is the Chalkiopoulo Lagoon.

selves. According to the most likely version of the story, the Corinthian expedition was led by Chesicrates, a member of the royal family of the Bacchiads, who had been forced to leave his homeland as a political exile. The Corinthian colony occupied the site known as Palaiopoli, to the south of the modern town of Corfu, between the bay of Garitsa and the Chalkiopoulou lagoon. Those two expanses of sea were the location of Corfu's twin harbours, the harbour of Alcinous and the Hyllaean harbour, respectively. However, even our finds from the eighth century BC are sparse, consisting mostly of shards of pottery from stratigraphic investigations.

We know from the literary sources that Corfu developed rapidly during the eighth and seventh centuries BC, acquiring wealth and naval strength thanks to its performance in the commercial sphere. In 710 BC, it founded

Ancient Cercyra was founded by the first colonists from Corinth between the Lagoon and Garitsa Bay.

its own first colony, at Croton in Lower Italy, and in 680 BC it expanded that territory with the founding of a second city, that of Locri. In collaboration with Corinth, and on its own initiative, it set up quite a number of other colonies in Lower Italy and much closer, on the coast of Epirus. However, its growing powerbrought it into conflict with its mother city, and in 664 BC Corfu and Corinth fought out what Thucydides described as the first sea battle in Greek history. This battle marked the beginning of a long period of antagonism between Corfu and Corinth. The conflict between the two cities focused largely on economic matters.

In the late seventh century BC, Periander, tyrant of Corith, managed to vanquish the island. His conquest opened an era of intensive building and artistic progress, under the influence of the Corinthian art which was then at its zenith. It was under Periander that the great temple of Artemis at Ayii Theodori was built, together with the superb circular cenotaph of Menecrates. After Periander's death, during the sixth century, the sanctuaries of Apollo Cercyraeus and of Hera were built, as was the temple to an unknown deity at Kardaki in the grounds of Mon Repos. Traces of residential dwellings of the same period have been discovered on the west side of the Kanoni promontory, the necropolis has come to light at Garditsa and on Sotiros hill, and the pottery found reveals connections not only with Corinth but also with Asia Minor, with which Corfu seems to have been trading as far back as the eighth century BC. Trade relations with quite a number of different areas led to significant growth, especially after Periander died and the island was free again. After the end of the seventh century BC, Corfu minted its own coins, and at the time of its greatest prosperity had a population of around 10,000, a huge number for a city of that time.

By the early fifth century BC, Corfu had a large fleet, and during the Persian Wars it was the second most powerful Greek naval power, surpassed only by Athens. It sent 60 triremes to the Battle of Salamis but, according to the account of the war given by Herodotus, they deliberately lingered on their journey so as not to arrive until after the out-

p. 28

An antefix of the Archaic period depicting the head of Medusa. From an unidentified building near the village of Afra.

come had been decided. Other narratives say the Corfiot fleet was delayed by bad weather as it circumnavigated the Peloponnese. Even so, the Corfiots were denounced by the Athenians, and supported only by Themistocles, commander of the forces of Athens, who may have been swayed by the size of the Corfiot fleet. Later, when he was exiled from Athens, he was able to take shelter on Corfu.

Another dispute between Corfu and Corinth was among the basic factors which triggered the Peloponnesian War in 431 BC, dividing the city-states of Greece into two armed camps, one led by Athens and the other by Sparta. The bone of contention between Corfu and Corinth was the colony of Epidamnus (now Dyrrachio/Durrazzo, on the coast of Albania), which the two cities had jointly founded in 627 BC. In 435, civil strife in Epidamnus led to the expulsion of the oligarchic party from the city and caused the democrats to seek the support of Corfu. When the Corfiots declined, the democrats of Epidamnus offered their city to Corinth, which sent a garrison to strengthen the colony's own troops. Corfu then laid siege to Epidamnus and successfully fought a naval battle against the fleet from Corinth. There was a second battle in 432 BC, also won by the Corfiots - though this time with the help of Athens. The

Athenian intervention caused displeasure in Corinth, which believed that this was tantamount to a breach of the peace agreement that Athens had earlier signed with the cities of the Peloponnese. Thus it was that the Peloponnesian War broke out. During the early years of the war, Corfu fought on the Athenian side, but subsequently the island became the theatre of savage civil strife between the democratic and oligarchic factions. Needless to say, both Athens and Sparta became involved in this civil war on the sides, respectively, of the democrats and the oligarchs. After a period of bloody warfare between 427 and 425 BC, the democrats prevailed; their first act was to put all their oligarchic opponents to death, and their second was to rejoin the Athenian alliance and send troops to the Sicilian expedition in 415 BC. By the end of the war, Corfu was exhausted and half the city's population was dead. In 375 BC, Sparta launched a fresh assault on Corfu, but the local troops beat them off, with help from Athens. Once again, Corfu found itself on the Athenian side in 338 BC, when the islanders fought bravely against Philip II of Macedon at the battle of Chaeroneia. All these operations in the fifth and fourth centuries BC led the Corfiots to build walls around their city, traces of which can still be seen at Ayii Theodori (the Nerantzicha tower) and by the harbour of Aliconous (remains of the east wall).

Under the Macedonians, the city, now considerably weakened, suffered from frequent raids. In 303 BC it was occupied by the Spartan general Cleomenes, and it was later besieged by Cassander of Macedon. In 299 BC, Corfu was given as a marriage gift to Pyrrhus, king of Epirus. After the failure of Pyrrhus' campaigns in Italy (280-275 BC), Corfu became an independent democratic state, but it attracted the attention of pirate gangs from Illyria, who laid siege to it in 229 BC and forced it to surrender. Throughout the third and second centuries BC the city of Corfu expanded steadily along the promontory now known as Kanoni, and it was divided up into a number of districts (*insulae*). Excavations have revealed quite a number of dwelling-houses dating from this period, sections of the elaborate drainage system, and tombs in the Hellenistic cemetery on the outskirts of the modern town.

2. THE ROMAN PERIOD (229 BC - 395 AD)

Illyrian rule over Corfu did not last long, because the Corfiots appealed for help to the Roman consul Fulvius, who managed to drive the pirates out. Then, in 229 BC, the island voluntarily surrendered to the Romans, who granted it complete autonomy and many privileges, on condition that they were allowed to use the ships and harbours of the island. Corfu thus became one of the most important Roman naval bases. Visitors included emperors and statesmen (Nero, Julius Caesar, Vespasian, Cicero) and also many rich Romans, who owned estates and luxurious villas there. During the Roman civil war of the first century BC, the Corfiots sided with Anthony and when he was defeated at Actium in 31 BC Octavian, the victor, wrecked the island. After many years of decline, Corfu began to prosper once again during the first and second centuries AD. As has been demonstrated by archaeological excavations, the city of Corfu was then confined to the environs of the two harbours and the Agora, although numerous baths, porticos and monuments to the heroes had been built in the meantime.

Under Tiberius or Claudius (probably around 48 AD), two of the disciples of St Paul, Saints Jason and Sosipater, preached Christianity on the island. Their names were later commemorated in a monumental church which can still be seen today in the island's capital. The Christians of Corfu were subjected to merciless persecution by the Roman Emperors, especially during the reign of Diocletian (284-305 AD).

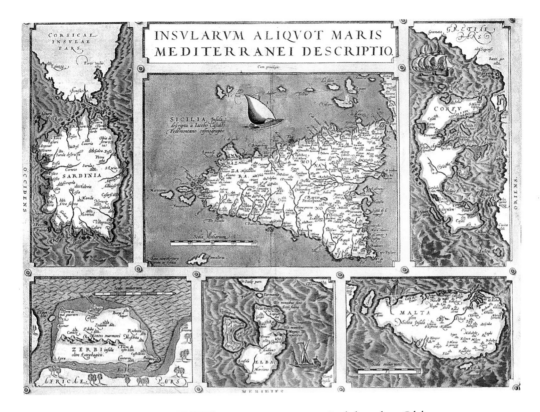

3. THE BYZANTINE PERIOD (395 - 1267)

When Theodosius split the Roman Empire into two parts in 395 AD, Corfu became part of the East Roman (or Byzantine) Empire. Between the fifth and the ninth centuries, it was frequently raided by barbaric tribes of Vandals, Goths and Saracens. The worst looting took place in 541, at the hands of Totilas, king of the Goths, during the course of a war between Byzantium and the Ostrogoths. It was about this time that the inhabitants began to move, little by little, towards the naturally strong site now occupied by the Old Fortress. The move seems to have been completed by the eleventh century. This new town with its twin peaks, was called Corypho and accounts for the name of the entire island in the Western languages.

Throughout the Byzantine period, Corfu belonged to the administrative *theme* of Cephalonia. In the ninth century, its Church became an archbishopric and was controlled directly by the Patriarchate of Constantinople. The fleet of Corfu took part in almost all the naval campaigns waged by the Byzantines, and the island soon developed into a most important trading-station and naval base. Its

p. 31

A copper engraving by A. Ortelius showing a map of six Mediterranean islands, from a book published in 1584.

Top right, Corfu.

strategic position on the western fringe of the Byzantine Empire made it a bastion against the attacks from the west which became menacing after the eleventh century. In 1081, the Norman baron Robert Guiscard and his son Bohemund captured Corfu and held it for four years. The islanders were able to shake off the Norman yoke quite a number of times, but the **Normans** returned in 1147, under Roger II of Sicily. In 1149, the Emperor Manuel Comnenus formed an alliance with the fleet of Venice and managed to subdue the Normans after many months of siege. The Normans recaptured Corfu for a short period in 1185, but they were soon expelled by Isaac Angelus.

Once back in Byzantine hands, Corfu seems to have gone through a period of prosperity. Its wealth attracted the attention of the notorious Genoese pirate **Vetrano Caffaro**, who after constant raids along the coast of the island finally occupied it in 1199. The Fourth Crusade of 1202-1204 led to the occupation of Constantinople by Western forces and the division of the Empire, as a result of which Corfu was ceded to Venice. Caffaro, however, refused to surrender power and a two-year siege was needed before his fleet could be defeated. Caffaro himself was executed as a warning to others. During the **first period of Venetian rule** (1207-1214), the territory of the island was split up into estates and divided among the

p. 33
The castle of Angelokastro, in the north of the island, was built in the thirteenth century and was one of Corfu's strongest defences against pirates.

Venetian nobles, who held their land in exchange for an annual tax payable to Venice and the obligation to defend the island when necessary. The Venetians were careful to grant the local people commercial privileges and to keep on good terms with them.

In 1214, Corfu came back into Greek hands; specifically, those of Michael I Angelus Ducas, who at this time set up the **Despotate of Epirus** or **Greece**, one of the three independent Greek states which emerged when the Crusaders overthrew the Byzantine Empire. The Corfiots gave an enthusiastic welcome to their fellow-Greek ruler, who rewarded them by guaranteeing all the privileges they already enjoyed and granting them additional ones. Particular importance was attached to the Church of Corfu, one of the twelve most important bishoprics in Greece. Under Archbishop Georgios Vardanis, known as 'Atticus', the privileges of the Church of Corfu were guaranteed by a silver bull issued in 1228. It was about this time that Angelokastro, a powerful fortress, was constructed in the north west of the island, where it did much to strengthen the defences of Corfu against pirates.

Michael I was succeeded in 1236 by Michael II, who retained the privileges already enjoyed by the islanders and the clergy and took care to ensure that the island was released from taxation. However, in a later attempt to lay claim to

the Imperial throne of Byzantium he made an alliance with **Manfred, Prince of Achaia and King of the Two Sicilies**, to whom he married his daughter - including Corfu among the lands which were given as the girl's dowry (1259). Manfred, in turn, ceded the island to his admiral, Philip Cinardus of Cyprus, and he made over some of its estates to Westerners ('Franks'). Manfred himself was defeated and killed at the battle of Venevento in 1266, and the victor, Charles I d'Anjou, king of Naples and the Two Sicilies, laid claim to Corfu - as indeed the Despot of Epirus had also done. But Cinardus refused to hand over what he regarded as his property, and so the Despot of Epirus had him murdered. The defence of the island was undertaken by Garnieri Alamano, who applied for assistance to Charles d'Anjou - and as a result Corfu became, in 1267, part of the empire of the Angevin dynasty of Naples.

4. THE ANGEVINS (1267 - 1386)

Angevin sovereignty was recognised at once by the deposed Latin emperor, and Charles I ceded the administration of the island to Garnieri Alamano, who was succeeded as high commissioner by Jordane de san Felice. The Angevins abolished the historic Orthodox bishopric of Corfu and replaced the bishop himself with a member of the lower clergy who bore the title of 'Great High Priest'. The cathedral and most of the parish churches were occupied by Latin priests, who were subject to a Latin archbishop. The land of the island was divided into four Bailiwicks: those of the Yiros (around the town), the Oros (the hilly area in the north), the Mesi (the centre of the island) and Lefkimmi, and a complete feudal system was introduced. Amid the general unrest and misfortune of the Angevin period, the Corfiots also had to deal with one disastrous pirate raid after another. The defences of the island were further strengthened with the construction of another castle, at Kassiope, but this was ruined by the Venetians before long.

In the late thirteenth century, King Charles II of Naples displayed some favour towards the inhabitants by granting them once more the privileges they had formerly enjoyed. In 1294, he ceded the island to Philip of Taras, on the occasion of the marriage of the latter to Thamar, daughter of the Despot of Epirus. Philip's name was remembered because of his conciliatory attitude towards the Corfiots - which did not, however, extend to the religious toleration they so wished. His successors, Robert and then Philip II (who gave a measure of freedom to the Orthodox clergy), behaved in a similar manner. After the death of Philip II, Joan, Queen of Naples ruled in Corfu, which was taken in 1380 by her nephew Philip II, James de Beau, and in 1382 by Charles III of Dyrrachium, who confirmed the islanders in their privileges.

Charles III held on to power until his death, but after that Corfu was without a sovereign lord and the barons split into a number of factions. In the midst of this general dynastic upheaval, Venice - which had always been interested in this prosperous island on its own doorstep - took the opportunity to acquire Corfu by peaceful means. In 1386, the Corfiots eventually resigned themselves to the prospect of Venetian rule, at a time when their city was under siege from Francesco Carrara, prince of Padua. The Angevins made sporadic attempts to recapture what had once been theirs, but they achieved little and in 1402 the Venetians sealed their conquest by purchasing the island from the kingdom of Naples for 30,000 gold ducats.

p. 35
An engraving of 1839-1841, from G.N. Wright's The Shores and Islands of the Mediterranean. Part of Corfu town and the Old Fortress can be distinguished.

5. THE SECOND PERIOD OF VENETIAN RULE (1386 - 1797)

The second period of Venetian rule lasted four centuries and was a most important era for Corfu in view both of the economic progress which took place at that time and of the assimilation of numerous elements in the mental makeup and culture of the Venetians which can still be detected today. Unlike the rest of Greece, most of which groaned under subjugation to the Turks, the Corfiots experienced the lighter hand of Venetian rule, partly as a result of the fact that co-operation between the local people and their masters was generally excellent. For the Venetians, the island was a bastion against the expansionism of the Ottoman Empire, with its designs on conquest in the West, and also a bridge across which their economic penetration of the East could be facilitated. As a result, they took particular care over the defence and fortification of Corfu: the island became the base of the admiral of the Venetian fleet, and for more than three centuries could have been called the Gibraltar of the Adriatic.

In the administrative field, the Venetians organised Corfu - and the other islands in the Ionian group - on a centralised system, although the local population

was accorded a degree of autonomy and the aristocrats enjoyed a number of privileges. The higher posts in the administration were, of course, held by Venetian noblemen, who were answerable only to the Supreme Council in Venice. This class of the *nobili*, which consisted largely of those who owned big estates, was a closed one in Corfu, under Venetian influence, and it was very hard for new members to gain admittance to it. After 1572, the names of all the aristocratic families were recorded in a special list known as the *Libro d'Oro* ('book of gold'). The urban middle class, called the *civili*, consisted principally of merchants and shipowners, who over the centuries acquired large fortunes and made attempts to enter the class of the nobility. The most oppressed class was that of the ordinary people, the *populari,* consisting of the farm and manual labourers, who were deprived of any civil rights and also had the responsibility of serving in the armed forces that were expected to defend the island.

Supreme administrative and judicial authority was vested in a single Venetian noble, the Vailos or Bailey. After 1420, he was assisted by two Councillors and the Providatore, the commander of the island's garrison. In the sixteenth century, administration of

pp. 36-37

A French woodcut of 1861 showing Corfu town and the twin peaks of the Old Fortress.

37

the island was taken over by the General Providatore of the East, who was responsible for all the Ionian islands and also for the navy that protected them. Corfiot nobles also took part in the administration of the island, side by side with the Venetians, forming a General Council which met once a year and elected the City Council. All the officials of state were appointed by this body.

The organisation of the Church in Corfu during the centuries of Venetian rule did not differ greatly from the conditions which the Angevins had established. However, the Venetians did not inter-

fere in Church affairs as long as they did not have political implications. Their friendly attitude towards the Orthodox Church was, of course, partly the result of their own desire to gain independence of the Pope, but they were always careful to control the degree of influence which the clergy had over the population of Corfu so as to prevent any upsurge of nationalist passions.

The economy of Venetian Corfu relied mostly on trade and farming. The Venetians were responsible, first and foremost, for developing the cultivation of the olive, in an attempt to rival the Genoese

p. 38
A copper engraving from A.G. de St. Sauver's Voyage historique dans les îsles Venetiennes du Levant (1801); a masterly depiction of the rare subject of the village of Gouvia and its harbour.

in the olive oil market. It was they who took the initiative in fostering the cultivation of the olive which still flourishes on the island today (see POSITION - GEOGRAPHY - ECONOMY). Trade, too, was a significant source of income for the Venetians, and it burgeoned thanks to the vital position occupied by the harbour of Corfu: through it, goods could be moved from East to West and vice versa. However, almost the entire burden of making the economy work was borne by the farming population, who were obliged to work in shocking conditions and lacked any entitlement either to a voice in politics or to education.

Although the Corfiots maintained peaceful co-operation with the Venetians, the period of Venetian rule was very far from a peaceful one, thanks to the hostile disposition of the neighbouring states. Genoa, whose power rivalled that of Venice in earlier times, twice attacked Corfu: once in 1403, when its forces wreaked havoc along the west coast of the island, and again in 1432, when it raided and besieged parts of the island close to the city. Of course, the greatest menace of all were the Turks, who after conquering almost all of the Greek mainland frequently

p. 39
A view of the Old Fortress, Corfu, from Christopher Wordsworth's Greece (1853).

attempted to capture the Venetian-occupied territories as well. Their first attack on Corfu was launched in the time of Bayazid II, and the town was only saved by turning the houses of the outlying suburbs into makeshift fortificatory works (1431).

In the reign of Suleiman the Magnificent, when the Ottoman Empire and Venice were in a constant state of war, Hair-ed-Din Barbarossa, an Algerian pirate in the Sultan's service, frequently raided the country areas of Corfu and in 1537 he laid siege to the town itself with a force of 25,000 men. All the Corfiots rallied to the defence of their city and drove the Turks off; Barbarossa was recalled to Constantinople. With him, unfortunately, he took several thousand Corfiot prisoners, who were sold in the slave markets of the East.

Further unsuccessful attempts were launched by the Turks in 1571 and 1573, at which point the Venetians decided that the time had come to built yet another castle, the New Fortress, and to strengthen the city walls. This proved to be a particularly good idea, because the Turks returned to the attack in 1716, during the last Turkish-Venetian war. Under the command of Austrian general Matthias von Schulenberg, the combined Corfiot and Venetian forces succeeded in beating off the assaults of the Ottoman fleet, and proceeded to celebrate a victory which they believed was won thanks to the intervention of St Spyridon, patron saint of the island. Even today, the anniversary of the Turkish attack, on 11 August, is commemorated with church services of thanksgiving in honour of St Spyridon.

Apart from these external threats, the Venetians also had to deal with numerous internal problems, especially during the seventeenth century. In 1610, the landless peasants rose in revolt, refusing to turn over to the landowners the share of the harvest that was traditionally theirs. Thirty years later, their uprising was still more dynamic in form: they occupied the palace of the Bailey and released from the prison in the Old Fortress all those who had been imprisoned for debt. This revolt, and the two which followed in 1642 and 1652, were suppressed by the dynamic intervention of the Venetian army. War, civil disturbance, and devastating epidemics of the plague in 1629 and 1673 brought about a drastic reduction in the population of Corfu.

Throughout Venetian rule, the authorities attempted to resolve this demographic problem by permitting new settlers, most of them refugees from the Turkish-occupied mainland, to establish themselves on the island. Corfu thus became a place of refuge for people from Constantinople, Epirus, Nafplio (after 1540) and

Crete (after 1669). As a rule, these new arrivals settled in villages which they themselves founded: Anaplades, Nafpliotes, Kritika, Argyrades and Ayios Markos (Cretans) were established in this way. The immigrants included many scholars and artists, who made the island the first place in the east into which the Italian Renaissance had penetrated. In 1461, the refugees included Thomas Palaeologus, the last Despot of the Peloponnese, and his family.

6. THE FIRST PERIOD OF FRENCH RULE (1797 - 1799)

By the eighteenth century, the Most Serene Republic of Venice was obviously in decline. The Venetian state was overthrown by Napoleon Bonaparte, who rapidly developed an interest in the strategic significance of the Ionian islands. In 1797, General Gentily occupied Corfu, and by the Treaty of Campo Formio the Ionian islands were included

p. 41
The New Fortress, Corfu; woodcut from The Illustrated London News (1863).

within the sovereignty of the republican French. The Corfiots greeted their new masters with enthusiasm, under the influence of the teachings of the French Revolution and in the belief that the lower classes would receive more just treatment. The *Libro d'Oro* was burned in the main square of the town and the coats-of-arms of the nobles, whether Corfiot or Venetian, were defaced.

The French placed the administration of the island in the hands of what was called the Democratic City Council, which included representatives of the middle classes as well as of the aristocracy. However, these new rulers, too, were unable to quell the displeasure of the Corfiots, upon whom they imposed heavy taxation and compulsory loans. They also disarmed the people and behaved with barbarous disrespect towards their religious monuments. Yet the French did make some important contributions to the life of the island, introducing a system of primary education and founding the first printing-house in what was later to become Greece.

7. RUSSO - TURKISH OCCUPATION
THE SEPTINSULAR STATE
(1799 - 1807)

While French occupation lasted, it had the effect of driving Russia and Turkey into one another's arms and causing them to take action against France. In 1799, a joint Russo-Turkish fleet commanded by admirals Usakov and Kandir Bey captured Corfu after fighting which went on for four months. Under the Treaty of Constantinople, signed on 21 March 1800 by Russia, Turkey and Britain, all the Ionian islands were formed into what became

known as the Septinsular Republic, which was recognised by the European Powers and survived until 1807. The Republic, whose capital was Corfu, enjoyed autonomy in return for tribute paid to the Ottoman Empire. One of the representatives of the Septinsular Republic at Constantinople was Ioannis Capodistrias, who was later to become the first Governor of the independent Greek state.

The basic administrative organ of the Septinsular Republic was the Senate, consisting of 14 representatives from all the islands. The new constitution adopted at this time gave the nobles all the privileges which they had formerly enjoyed, causing the general

p. 43

One of the main streets in the commercial centre of Corfu town, with impressive mansions and churches. Engraving from G.N. Wright's The Shores and Islands of the Mediterranean (1839).

displeasure of all the other sections of the population. In 1801, after the *popolari* had risen in revolt, Spyridon Theotokis, President of the Ionian Senate, carried out a revision of the Constitution, but his initiative met with opposition from the European Powers. It was not until 1806 that a new constitution for the Ionian islands could be ratified, and even it went no further than to place the Septinsular Republic under the protection of Russia. As a result, the islands lost such autonomy as they had had and during the Russo-Turkish war which followed they were obliged to fight on the Russian side.

p. 44
View of Corfu; from G.N. Wright's The Shores and Islands of the Mediterranean (1839).

8. SECOND PERIOD OF FRENCH RULE (1807 - 1814)

In 1807, Russia and France signed the Treaty of Tilsit, by which the Ionian islands were granted to Napoleon and became provinces of France. During this second period of rule, the French took a particular interest in the intellectual and economic development of Corfu: they founded the Ionian Academy (1808), which for the first time allowed the lower classes some scope for education, they re-organised the civil service, they introduced compulsory military service, they laid out the street

plan of Corfu town, they constructed many new buildings and landscaped the Spianada in the centre of town, and they introduced new crops, such as potatoes and tomatoes.

French rule over Corfu lasted only seven years, since in the meantime the British had managed to detach large sections of the French Empire from the mother-state and had seriously weakened Napoleon. When Napoleon finally fell in 1814, and after the Congresses of Vienna and Paris, the Ionian islands were placed under British protection, but did not become colonies either of Britain or of Austria, which had also had designs upon them.

9. THE BRITISH PROTECTORATE (1816 - 1864)

When the French, too, evacuated their islands, the Corfiots hoped that they would at last gain their independence. Ioannis Capodistrias actually submitted a proposal to that effect to the Congress of Vienna, but Britain, Austria and Prussia vetoed it. Capodistrias also intervened in the Congress of Paris, this time to much more effect since he was able to prevent the complete subjugation of the islands to Britain. The Paris Treaty of 1815 recognised a United

p. 45

Corfu town as seen from the islet of Vido. Woodcut from The Illustrated London News (1861).

10. UNION WITH GREECE (1864)

After many years of effort, the Ionian islands were incorporated into the Greek state on 21 May 1864. However, Britain did not make this concession without taking political considerations into account: it was Britain which insisted that a Danish prince whom it trusted be installed, at the same time, as King George I of Greece. After the treaty of unification was signed, the Ionian islands were compelled

States of the Ionian Islands, as a free entity under British control. Corfu remained the capital of the state, which was administered by a British High Commissioner.

The first High Commissioner, Sir Thomas Maitland, soon clashed with Capodistrias over the oppressive policies which Britain was exercising in the islands, but he refused to carry out the revision of the Constitition which Capodistrias proposed. It was not until 1848 that the Constitution was revised, granting freedom of the press and immediately leading to the publication of the first newspaper of Corfu. Greek was also recognised for the first time as the official language of state, and a system of education was set up. Lord Frederick Guildford took the initiative, in 1824, of founding a new Ionian Academy, which was in effect the first Greek university. Corfu also has the British to thank for its water supply system and for the good road network, for which Sir Frederick Adam was responsible.

to demolish all their fortifications, while Corfu and Paxoi were declared neutral territory.

However, the neutrality of Corfu proved on a number of occasions to be something of a formality. During the First World War, Entente forces landed Serbian and French troops on the island, and in early 1916 the Serbian government-in-exile established itself there. A year later, Serbian Prime Minister Pasic and South Slav representative Trubic signed what was known as the 'Corfu declaration', which laid the foundations for the formation of Yugoslavia by the Serbs, the Croats and the Slovenians.

Corfu's neutrality was violated once more in 1923, when the Italians, holding Greece responsible for the assassination of the Italian general Tallini, bombed the island and occupied it. The Italians bombed Corfu once again when the Second World War broke out, and later, in 1943, it was raided mercilessly by the Germans, who occupied it and remained in control of it until the end of the war in 1945.

p. 47
Vlacherna Monastery and Pontikonisi; French woodcut of 1877.

CORFU TOWN DOWN THE CENTURIES

1. ANCIENT CORFU

T he first colonists who settled on Corfu, from Eretria, established their city in the eighth century BC at the head of the **Hyllaean harbour**, now known as the Chalkiopoulo lagoon and occupied by Corfu airport. It was between that harbour, which took its name from Hyllus, son of Heracles, and the **harbour of Alcinous**, in the part of town now known as Anemomylos, that the Corinthians under Chesicrates set up their colony. Little by little, the city expanded south towards Figareto and occupied almost all of the promontory called Kanoni.

Literary references, and in particular the description given by Thucydides in Book III of his *Histories*, and archaeological excavations allow us to form a clear picture of the city of Cercyra as it must have been during and after the Classical period. We also know quite a lot about the earlier monuments in the area.

After the fifth/fourth century BC, Cercyra was protected by walls, of which very little has survived. The north wall must have run from one harbour to the other, while the south wall was in the vicinity of Figareto. Excavations have revealed the ruins of the **Nerantzicha tower**, part of the north wall, at Ayii Theodori, and sections of the south wall. Archaeologists have also discovered the more easterly of the two towers which protected the harbour of Alcinous (at Anemomylos, beneath the chapel of St Athanasius). The **acropolis** must have been on one of the hills in the Analipsi area, while the **private dwelling-houses** would have been located to the north-west, at Figareto, as can be concluded from the traces of houses, streets and pipe systems found there. The ancient city's water supply came from the **Kardaki**

p. 49

The Nerantzicha Tower, part of the north wall of ancient Cercyra, as it survives today in the Ayii Theodori district of the town.

spring, along an aqueduct located in the vicinity of the Nerantzicha tower.

The **Agora** of ancient Cercyra was at **Palaiopoli**, very close to the Mon Repos estate; it would have consisted of public buildings, sanctuaries, porticoes, workshops and baths, but very few traces of these structures have come down to us. However, excavations have revealed the remains of a **baths**, dating from Roman times and ornamented with mosaic floors and statues, sections of a magnificent **portico** and a **semicircular building**, a **Roman balaneum** and some parts of **harbour works** which were in use from the Archaic period down to Roman times.

Mon Repos

Many important monuments have been excavated in the **Mon Repos estate**, an area of 24 hectares which after 1830 contained the summer palace of the British High Commissioner. Later, it was made over to the Greek royal family, and it now belongs to the Greek state. Since 1994, the Municipality of Corfu has been responsible for the estate, which is now open to the public. In 1822, a team of British workmen who were trying to find out why the Kardaki spring had run dry accidentally discovered the **Kardaki temple**, the best-preserved temple on the island. This is a Doric peripteral structure with

pp. 50-51
The Kardaki temple in the Mon Repos estate. In the illustration, the Doric columns of the long sides of the temple, the pronaos and the cella with the altar in ts interior.

several Ionic features, with six monolithic columns along each of its short sides and eleven on each of the long sides. The temple measured 25 metres by 12. There is a *pronaos* and a *cella,* inside which was found an enormous altar. It seems likely that this altar already stood on the site and was incorporated into the temple when it was constructed in the late sixth century BC. When the altar is located inside the temple, it is an indication that the building was dedicated to chthonic (underworld) deities, but in this case we do not know the name of the god in question although votive offerings to Poseidon and Apollo have been found. The building seems to have been destroyed in the late second century BC, and a cult of Cybele later sprang up on the site: a statue of the goddess was found in one corner of the building. Beneath the temple is a cave, which seems to communicate with the altar in the *cella,* but excavation beyond the point reached is almost impossible because of the weight of the surviving structure.

Also within the Mon Repos estate is the famous **sanctuary of Hera**, which Thucydides refers to in his account of the civil war on the island. Its position has been identified by the finding of a boundary marker dating from the second half of the fifth century BC, which mentions the sanctuary and refers to Hera with the epithet Acraea - 'of the peak'. The trench in which the foundations of the temple were located, votive offerings, and some architectural members have also survived. It would seem from the finds that the temple was founded in the late seventh century BC and reconstucted at least three times before its final destruction by Agrippa in the first century BC. This was the largest and most important temple in the ancient city of Cercyra.

Close to the sanctuary of Hera, traces have come to light of another sanctuary, dedicated to Apollo Cercyraeus. Indeed, the Mon Repos estate is one enormous archaeological site; under the scheme for the unification of the archaeological sites of Corfu town, the area will be landscaped so that it forms a park where other activities will be housed apart from the antiquities. The palace building in the centre of the estate will be converted into a museum to house the finds from Palaiopoli.

p. 52
View of the Kardaki temple (late sixth century BC).

The temple of Artemis

Near the Hyllaean harbour in the Ayii Theodori district of Corfu town, archaeologists have discovered another temple of the greatest importance. This is the temple of Artemis, some parts of which were found by French soldiers in 1812 when a moat was being dug. The west pediment of the temple has survived in excellent condition; it shows the Gorgon Medusa, and is the earliest such depiction to have come down to us from antiquity (see Corfu Archaeological Museum). The temple of Artemis, which would appear from the theme of the pedimental sculpture to have been conventionally known as the temple of the Gorgon, was built in limestone around 590-580 BC. It was in the Doric order and pseudo-dipteral (that is, the distance between the perimetric columns and the main temple is sufficient to admit the existence of a second perimetric colonnade on the inner side), with eight columns on each of the short sides and 17 on each of the long sides. The temple is unusually elongated (measuring 22.40 x 47.60 metres), and had a *pronaos*, a *cella* and an *opisthodomos*. The cella was divided into three aisles by two lateral

p. 53

View of the sanctuary of Artemis at Ayii Theodori; a retaining wall supporting the Hellenistic stoa.

double (two-storeyed) colonndes, each of ten columns. Apart from the west pediment, the sculptures from some of the triglyphs and the metopes have survived, together with a terracotta *sima* and a marble *sima* which seems to have replaced the terracotta member around 530 BC. There was also a huge altar with a length of 25 metres, ornamented with triglyphs and metopes.

Close to the temple of Artemis, traces have been found of a temple dedicated to Pythian Apollo and dating from the fifth century BC. In addition to the temples already identified, the literary sources tell us of many more temples and sanctuaries which must have stood somewhere in ancient Cercyra: those of Zeus, Poseidon, Hermes, Asclepius, Heracles, Castor and Pollux and Alcinous. The constant raids and sackings of the island can be assumed to have been responsible for the desecration of these monuments. In addition, building materials from most of the temples was removed during the Byzantine period and used for the construction of new Christian churches.

The ancient necropolis

The archaeologists have managed to discover quite a quantity of information about the position of the necropolis of ancient Cercya, which lay directly adjacent to the city by a long sandy beach outside the north walls, near the harbour of Alcinous (at modern Garitsa, on the southern slopes of Sotiros hill). Finds confirm that the necropolis was in use as far back as the second half of the seventh century BC, and the grave goods found in the tombs reflect the existence of a city which was advanced both in terms of the items it could manufacture and the trade relations it maintained. Most of the burials involved the placing of the corpse directly in the ground, though burials in jars have also been found, as have traces of cremation, cist tombs, stone sarcophagi and stone funerary monuments.

The most important find to have come to light in the ancient necropolis is the famous **monument of Menecrates**, discovered by the British in 1843 when public works were being carried out. This is a circular funerary monument - actually, a cenotaph, constructed in 600 BC in memory of Menecrates. Menecrates, from the city of Oeantheia near modern Galaxidi on the north shore of the Gulf of Corinth, was the consul of Corfu in his native city, and he lost his life at sea. The monument consists of a circular tumulus of earth surrounded, up to the top, by a built perimetric wall. An Archaic inscription - running from right to left at the top of the wall - tells us about the family origins and profession of Menecrates, and states the manner of his death. Also in 1843, a lion statue was found here, and according to one theory (which is, however, not generally accepted) the lion may have stood on top of the cenotaph of Menecrates.

During the Hellenistic period, the necropolis of Corfu seems to have been moved in the direction of the Hyllaean harbour, on the south slopes of Sotiros hill near the modern airport. Excavations in the area have revealed very few traces of buildings but a large number of highly-concentrated and carefully constructed funerary stelae ('tombstones'). All these are in local limestone and they cover the whole range of *stelae* known in the Hellenistic period (simple rectangular stones with inscriptions, others with paintings, stones topped with pediments, monuments in the shape of miniature temples, etc.). The **Hellenistic necropolis** must have been destroyed by Agrippa in 31 BC, while the *stelae* from the tombs may have been assembled at some later point in antiquity and set aside to be used as materials for new buildings.

p. 55
The circular monument of Menecrates in the cemetery of Garitsa (600 BC).

CORFU ARCHAEOLOGICAL MUSEUM

p. 56

A Roman lantern with an ornamental relief.

p. 57

A lion statue which topped a funerary monument in the Garitsa cemetery (late seventh century BC).

C orfu Archaeological Museum, built in 1962-1965, stands on the corner of Vraila and Dimokratias Sts, on the boulevard at Garitsa, and has an interesting collection of finds from all over the island covering the period from the Palaeolithic era to Roman times.

In the **antechamber on the ground floor** are the following exhibits:

- **1985**: Part of a Roman Corinthian column capital from Palaipoli - **146**: A marble female torso of the late second century BC, in the well-known 'Maiden of Heracleio' type attributed to the sculptor Praxiteles (fourth century BC).

- **258**: A marble urn for funerary ashes, of the Roman period - **837**: Part of a Corinthian column capital from a funerary monument - **1984**: The marble base of a sprinkler - **140**: Roman bust of a woman - **1248**: Terracotta funerary amphora, fifth century BC.

- **141**: Marble bust of Faustina the Younger, wife of the Roman Emperor Marcus Aurelius (130-175 AD).

- **205**: Statue base with a depiction of the Rape of Persephone in relief (first century AD). Apart from Kore and Pluto, Artemis, Athena, (?) Demeter and Hermes can also be identified - **168**: Votive relief showing the goddess Cybele, represented twice.

The **antechamber on the upper floor** contains finds from the

p. 58

A funerary urn of the sixth century BC, from the cemetery at Garitsa.

ancient necropolis at Garitsa:
- **1914**: Large terracotta funerary urn of the sixth century BC
- **Case 1**: pottery of the seventh and sixth centuries BC made in Corinth and other Greek cities, but also including samples of local pottery which reveal the efforts of the Corfiots to compete with the potters of Corinth, especially during the late sixth century BC. - **3**: Elaborate Doric capital from a column surmounting the tomb of Xembares (first half of the sixth century BC), as noted in an inscription on its *abacus* - **2**: Funerary *stele* of Arnias, who as the inscription tells us was killed in a battle on the river Arachthus (early sixth century BC).

The most important exhibits in the **south hall** are as follows:
- **Case 2**: Pottery, flint blades, stone and copper tools of the prehistoric period, from Sidari and Grava near Gardiki (upper shelf), from Ermones (middle

shelf) and from Afionas and Kefali (lower shelf).

- **Case 3**: Terracotta vases of Corinthian origin and local pottery imitating Corinthian ware, seventh and sixth centuries BC (wine jugs, oil-flasks, alabasters, scent-holders, boxes).

- **Case 4**: Terracotta vases of the seventh and sixth centuries BC, from Garitsa (wine jugs, alabasters, boxes, oil-flasks, cups, cylixes).

- **Case 5**: Lead tablets incised with inscriptions relating to the debts of private citizens. From the Olive Oil Institute site in Palaiopoli (late sixth - early fifth century BC).

- **Case 6**: Terracotta statuettes and figurines of the sixth and fifth centuries BC, from various parts of the island. Note the statuettes of Artemis (upper shelf) and a terracotta vase with a depiction in relief of the Judgement of Paris (no. 260).

- **Case 7**: Bronze items, includ-

p. 59
The famous lion from the Garitsa cemetery (late seventh century BC).

ing a statuette of a warrior of 440 BC from Afionas (no. 558) and a statuette of a nude youth from North Epirus, dating from the fifth century BC (no. 1634); note also the black and red-figure pottery from Attica.

- **Case 8**: Two bronze consular inscriptions conferring honours on those who have served the city (fourth century BC).

- **Cases 24-25**: Silver and copper coins from Corfu and other parts of Greece (sixth - third centuries BC). - **1976**: In the centre of the gallery stands an outstanding **lion statue** found close to the circular cenotaph of Menecrates and believed by some to have surmounted it. However, this view is no longer accepted and experts believe that it must have stood on a rectangular tomb. The lion dates from the late seventh century BC and is the work of a Corinthian sculptor who worked in Corfu

(since the statue is in local limestone).

The animal is depicted with plain lines, in a crouching position and with a fierce expression, as if about to leap on its prey. This is one of the most striking depictions of a lion created during Greek antiquity.

The most important gallery in the museum is the **Gorgon hall**, dominated by the **west pediment of the temple of Artemis** found at Ayii Theodori. This is the earliest stone pediment to have survived from the art of ancient Greece, dating from 590-580 BC. It impresses us with its sheer size (length 17.02 m., central height 3.18 m.) and also with the subject and the careful manner of its rendition, demonstrating the level of skill which the artists of Corinth had reached even in those early times.

In the centre of the pediment, shown full-face, is a huge, demonic

pp. 60-61

The most striking exhibit in Corfu Museum is the pediment from the temple of Artemis Gorgo. The demon Gorgo, in the centre of the pediment, is flanked by Chrysaor (right) and Pegasus (left) and protected by two feline creatures (590-580 BC).

female figure, the lower half of whose torso is, strangely enough, half-turned to the right, giving us the impression that she is running (a pose typical of Archaic times). On her feet are winged sandals, and wings also sprout from her back. Her short tunic is caught at the waist with a pair of intertwined snakes. The curls of her hair also end in snakes. The face is monstrous, with huge ears and nose, bulging eyes and an open, evil mouth from which the tongue protrudes between sharp teeth. This female figure is none other than the Medusa, one of the Gorgons of Greek mythology, who we are told could turn to stone anyone who happened to see her terrible head. According to Hesiod, she was one of the three Gorgons who lived beyond Ocean, and she lost her life when Perseus decapitated her with the assistance of Athena and Hermes. The head was given to Athena and remained forever fixed to the goddess's shield. As she was being beheaded, Chrysaor and Pegasus, her two children from her union with Poseidon, sprang from the truncated throat. In this scene we see Chrysaor, in the form of a nude *kouros* of the Archaic era, to the Medusa's right, while on the left the rear of Pegasus - the famous untameable winged

horse of the myths - has survived.

The fact that the figure of Perseus is absent from this scene, while the Medusa is shown alive and in triumph together with her children, has led scholars to surmise that the purpose of the Corinthian artist was not to illustrate the myth of Hesiod but to attribute another dimension to this demonic creature. It may very well be that what we are seeing is a symbolic scene designed to accentuate the Medusa's ability to create life even out of death, associating her forces with the omnipotence of nature. The Medusa may have been one of the many facets of the Great Goddess of nature, who survived in ancient Greek thought from the prehistoric era down to Hellenistic times. This goddess rules over the earth and also the air, as we can see from the snakes and wings on her body, while she is also capable of taming wild nature and the fierce animals.

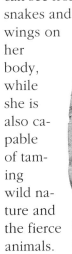

p. 62

Bronze statue of a youth running with a rhyton (570 BC).

p. 63

A rainwater spout in the shape of a lion's head, found at Mon Repos and probably from the temple of Hera (late seventh century BC).

This capacity is revealed in the depiction of the Medusa between two wild felines which are neither lions nor leopards but a combination of both. 'Mistress of the animals' is a frequent term of reference to Artemis, to whom the temple was dedicated. It may well be, then, that in this depiction of a Gorgon we see a sym-

bolic reference to one of the aspects of the nature of Artemis Gorgo, the deity whose cult was housed in the temple.

The two corners of the pediment are filled with scenes from various myths. On the right is Zeus during the Battle of the Titans, hurling his thunderbolt at the Titan Iapetus, while on the

p. 64
Head of a kouros from Mon Repos; an outstanding example of Archaic sculpture (530 BC).

left Poseidon, during the same battle, is attacking with his sword a seated figure who might be either Cronus or Rhea. A wall behind the seated figure might symbolise the Tower of the Blessed, where Cronus dwelt after the gods were victorious in the Battle of the Titans. This left-hand scene has, however, been interpreted in another way: the figure on the throne has been seen as Priam before the walls of Troy, at the moment of his murder by Neoptolemus.

The bottom of the cornice of the pediment is ornamented with a Greek-key motif in relief, while along the two lateral sections are incised ornamental fish and

p. 65

A limestone pediment from Figareto showing a scene from a banquet or a funeral dinner (500 BC).

flowers. The entire pediment would undoubtedly have been painted, but the paint has disappeared over the centuries. Stylistically, the composition is typically Archaic, with frontally-viewed, stylistic figures and highly ornamented individual features. The details are incised, the bodies are massive and squared-off, and the composition as a whole is notable for its austerity, as are all the works of the studios of the Peloponnese during the period in question. Even so, the vitality and power of the composition despite the simplicity of its expressive media make it a unique work.

Of the other sculptures that ornamented the temple of Artemis, only fragments of the east pediment have survived, along with part of a relief frieze showing a warrior (no. 1982, according to one interpretation a depiction of Achilles and Memnon), a painted terracotta *sima* with relief ornamentation (590-580 BC) and part of a marble *sima* which must have replaced its terracotta prede cessor around 533-525 BC.

More interesting exhibits are to be seen in the **north hall** of the Museum. Most of them were found during excavations at Mon Repos: **MR 773**: An antefix and rainwater spout in the shape of a lion's head, from the sanctuary of Hera - **MR 730**: An antefix in the shape of a Gorgon's head, from the sanctuary of Hera.

- **Case 11**: Statuettes, figurines, small terracotta vases and other items dating from the Archaic period and the fifth century BC.

- **MR 818**: A terracotta female head, probably a temple antefix (mid-sixth century BC).

- **Case 12**: Terracotta statuettes, busts, reliefs, masks and vases, of the seventh and sixth centuries BC - **MR 732**: A limestone head from a *kouros*, superb work by a Corinthian artist who worked in Corfu (535-530 BC).

- **1602**: A bronze statue of a reveller, a youth running with a *rhyton* in his hands, part of the ornamentation on a bronze kettle. This again is superb work, by a Laconian studio of around 570 BC - **Case 21**: Bronze finds of the period from the Geometric age to the fifth century BC.

- **Case 22**: Bronze finds from the sanctuary of Apollo Cercyraeus - **Case 20**: Bronze items, including a tiny lion from an ornamen-

pp. 66-67
Finds from a burial at the village of Prodromi, Thesprotia.
Below: the helment of the dead warrior. Facing page: his bronze corselet (late fourth - early third century BC).

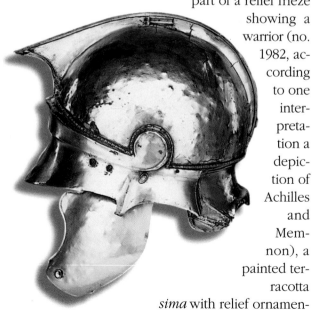

tal tripod (MR 477, sixth century BC). - **2297**: This hall is dominated by the left-hand section of a limestone pediment of 500 BC, found at Figareto. It probably shows a scene from a symposium or a funerary banquet, attending which are two men reclining on couches. One of them is beardless and holds a *cylix*, while the other is bearded and is holding a horn-shaped drinking mug. In front of them, on a different plane, are a helical *krater*, a dog of the Molossian type, and a feline creature which is lying beneath an elaborate table. All the figures are looking to the right, where the scene would undoubtedly have

continued. The bearded figure has been connected with the god Dionysus because of the iconographic elements associated with him and frequently found in portrayals of the deity (the horn, the animal skin cast over his shoulder, the feline creature which reminds us of the panther of Dionysus). The scene has thus been read as a Dionysiac symposium and has been interpreted as belonging to a temple of Dionysus at Figareto. From the stylistic features we can deduce the existence of a studio on Corfu which was under the influence of Corinthian art.

- **Case 13**: Statuettes, busts, fig-

p. 68
Prehistoric
terracotta vase
from Ermones.

urines and vases in terracotta, of the sixth and fifth centuries BC. Note the statuette of Hermaphroditus (MR 139) and a statuette of a flute-player, probably Pan (MR 640).

- **Case 14**: Terracotta items, mostly Megarian *scyphoi* with relief ornamentation of the third or second century BC and statuettes of the Hellenistic period.

- **Central case**: Finds from a tomb at the village of Prodromi in Thesprotia on the mainland: two helmets, a breastplate, a sword, and a scraper for removing olive oil from the skin (no. 7672), a key, a bronze funerary urn containing the ashes of the dead man, and two gilt wreaths of myr-

tle and oak (late fourth - early third century BC). - **Case 19**: Terracotta statuettes of Artemis from the so-called 'little sanctuary' of the goddess at Kanoni (late sixth - early fifth century BC).

- **Case 18**: Fragments of statuary from the pediment of an unidentified small temple in the ground of Mon Repos. The theme of the Battle of the Amazons has been recognised on at least one of the fragments.

- **153**: The torso of an Eros of the Praxitelean type (fourth century BC) - **152**: Torso of a nude god, possibly a copy of a bronze original by the sculptor Phidias, located on the Acropolis of Athens and showing Apollo Panorpius

p. 69

Wide terracotta vessel with spout, decorated in the black - figure technique (c. mid - sixth century BC).

(second century BC).

- **Cases 15, 16, 17**: Finds from the Late Hellenistic and Roman periods, from Palaiopoli and Kassiopi - **135**: Portrait of the historian Thucydides (300 BC) - **169**: Votive relief of Asclepius and Hygiea pouring libations at an altar and accompanied by a cult devotee (380-370 BC) - 133: Portrait of the Athenian comedy-writer Menander (fourth-third century BC), an outstanding Roman copy of a bronze original created by Cephisodotus and Timarchus, sons of Praxiteles. - 352: Part of a votive relief showing Zeus Meilichius (fourth century BC).

- **134**: Portrait of the philosopher Pyrrhon of Elis (200 BC).

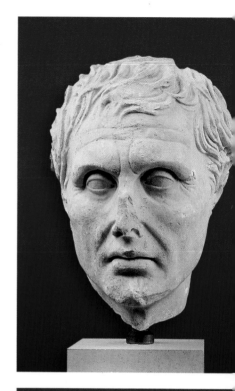

pp. 70-71

Above: head of a statue of the poet Menander (first century AD).

Terracotta statuette of Artemis, from the goddess's little sanctuary near Kanoni (480 BC).

Below: relief with a scene from a funeral banquet (third century BC).

Right: statue of Apollo, of what is called the 'Kassel type' (second century BC).

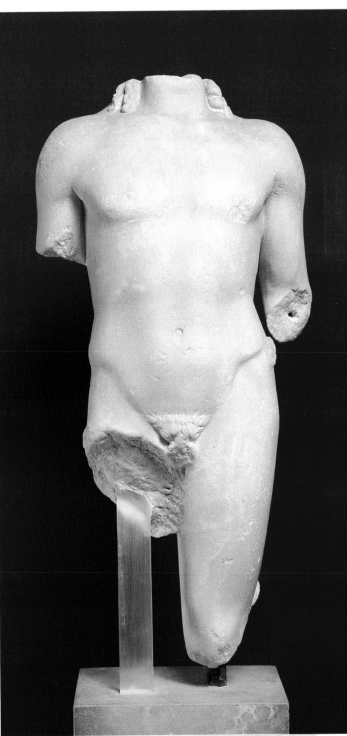

2. THE BYZANTINE TOWN

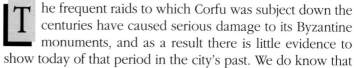

p. 72

St Cyril of Alexandria; icon painted by Emmanouil Tzanes in 1654 (Antivouniotissa Museum).

The frequent raids to which Corfu was subject down the centuries have caused serious damage to its Byzantine monuments, and as a result there is little evidence to show today of that period in the city's past. We do know that in the sixth century, after the raids of the Goths, the ancient city was abandoned and the inhabitants settled on the **promontory of the Old Fortress**. The move was completed by the eleventh century, and the new Byzantine town remained on the site until 1588. This area was called 'ton Coryfon', 'of the peaks', and this was the origin of the name 'Corfu' which town and island bear today in the western languages. In the tenth century the inhabitants built a wall around one of the peaks on the promontory, on the site where the Venetians later constructed the Sea Tower (Torre de Mare). Those who lived inside the fortress were called 'kastrinoi', 'castle-dwellers', and the part of Corfu which lay outside the wall, where the modern town now stands, was called **Exopolion** or **Xopoli**, 'the outer city'. Inside the fortress, the Corfiots built an Orthodox cathedral church to Sts Peter and Paul, but in the thirteenth century this was taken over by the Angevins and became a Latin church.

The Basilica of Palaiopoli

Long before the move to the Old Fortress took place, the Byzantines had erected a most important church of St Cercyra in the centre of the ancient city. The ruins of the church can still be seen today, in Palaiopoli, almost opposite the gate to the Mon Repos estate. The basilica of Palaiopoli, as it is known, was dedicated to St Cercyra, daughter of Cercyllinus, a Roman noble of Corfu, who was baptised Christian in 48 BC and martyred for her faith. The church had five aisles and was built in the fifth century,

p. 73-74
The church of St Cercyra - also known as the basilica of Palaiopoli - opposite the entrance to Mon Repos.

when Jovanus was archbishop, using materials from various ancient monuments, as we are told by an inscription on the epistyle. In the sixth century, the church was destroyed by the Vandals and Goths, and a smaller, three-aisled church was constructed in its place. This, in turn, was destroyed in the eleventh century and a third church, with only one aisle, was soon erected on the site. It was renovated in 1537. The church of St Cercyra was finally ruined by German bombing in 1943. Today, only sections of the outer walls have survived, and some of the architectural members and mosaics are kept in the Collection of Christian Art.

The church of Sts Jason and Sosipater

Another of the important Byzantine monuments of Corfu, the church of Sts Jason and Sosipater in the Anemomylos district of town, has survived in much better condition. The saints in question were two of the seventy disciples of Christ himself, a tradition tells us, and also disciples of St Paul. Jason was bishop of Tarsus and Sosipater of Iconium. In the time of Tiberius or Claudius (around 48 AD), they visited Corfu and converted the islanders to Christianity. Some scholars say that the tombs of the two saints were originally inside the church, and today there are conventional memorials to their interment on either side of the door in the iconostasis.

The church itself dates from around the year 1000, but inscriptions built into the walls on either side of the main entrance testify to the existence of a still earlier church on the site. These inscriptions also tell us that the church we see today was donated by a certain priest called Stephanos when Theophanes was Bishop of Corfu. No other historical information about either of these personages has survived.

The church is of the domed, cruciform architectural type, with two columns upon which part of the dome rests, the remainder being supported by the walls. There is a narthex, the nave and the sanctuary. The dome is octagonal and the east side of the sanctuary consists of three apses, of which the central apse is three-sided while the other two are semicircular. The upper part of the dome, the south wall, and the arms of the cross - with the exception of the north arm - have been reconstructed and the bell-tower is an addition, dating from Venetian times. The walls are constucted on the cloisonné system: that is, all four sides of the blocks of stone are surrounded by hori-

p. 75

The Byzantine church of Sts Jason and Sosipater, seen from the south-east.

zontal and vertical courses of brick. Architectural members from ancient monuments in the Palaiopoli area have been built into the lower parts of the walls. The ornamentation of the outer surfaces is supplemented with bands of dentils running around the arches of the doors and windows and with the terracotta, wedge-shaped ornaments typical of the period and called Cufic motifs.

The church is entered from the narthex through a tribellum (a structure with three apertures across which a curtain could be drawn). Inside are sculptures, shrines and a stone iconostasis dating from the time of Venetian rule. The inner walls must have borne wall-paintings, as can be seen from the few surviving fragments. Only one of these paintings has come down to us in good condition: it dates from the eleventh century and shows St Arsenius, a local Corfiot saint who was bishop of the island in the tenth century. There were also important icons, the work of the greater painter Emmanoul Tzanes Bounialis (1610-1690), an artist of the Cretan School. Today, the icons of Sts Jason and Sosipater, of Christ Enthroned, of Our Lady Hodeghetria, of St Gregorios Palamas and of St John Damascene are still in the church, while an icon of St Cyril, Patriarch of Alexandria, has been moved to the Antivouniotissa

Museum. All the icons date from 1649-1650 (see p. 109).

In the courtyard of the church is the tomb of Catherine Palaeologina, wife of Thomas Palaeologus, the last Despot of Mystras, who died in Corfu in 1462. Her robes, too, are kept inside the church.

pp. 76-77
The west elevation of the church of Sts Jason and Sosipater. The bell-tower was added in Venetian times.

The Christian collection

An interesting collection of works dating from the Byzantine period is housed in the Palace of St Michael and St George on the main square of Corfu town. It contains architectural sculptures and mosaic floors from the Early Christian period found in the basilica of Palaiopoli, wall-paintings from the church of St Nicholas at Kato Korakiana (eleventh, thirteenth and eighteenth centuries), etc.

3. THE VENETIAN CITY

T he form which the town of Corfu took during the Venetian period is of much greater importance for the present day, since it has remained fundamentally unchanged down the centuries and is largely responsible for the physiognomy of the town today. As we walk along the narrow alleyways of Corfu town (known as *kantounia*), pause in the tiny squares with their fountains and churches in the western style, pass through the arcades and beneath the wonderful mansions, and gaze at the castles and walls that rise in front of us, we have the feeling that time stopped in the Venetian era. All the features left by the ancient and Byzantine periods, all that foreign conquerors later added to the mosaic of the city, and all that the Corfiots themselves have invented blends harmoniously together without adulterating its primarily medieval identity, that which it owes to the Venetians.

During the Venetian period, the centre of the city continued to be in the area of the Old Fortress,

pp. 78-79
Among the most important fortifications erected by the Venetians were the walls of the Old Fortress, which have survived down to the present day. In the illustration, a view of the promontory occupied by the Old Fortress.

where it had moved back in the sixth century. Gradually, however, the town spread outside the existing walls and a densely-populated suburb called Borgo or Xopoli came into existence. The planning and architecture of the city adapted themselves to the military purposes of the Venetians, who wanted Corfu to be a bastion against the expansion of the Turks into Europe. For that reason, great care was taken over the works which defended the town and new walls and fortresses with towers, moats and ramparts were built.

p. 80
The bridge across which we enter the Old Fortress.

The Old Fortress

The first task facing the Venetians was to strengthen the Byzantine fortifications of the Old Fortress which lay at the centre of their city. In the fifteenth century they built two walls, one surrounding the twin peaks of the promontory and another one, at a lower level, providing protection from attack by sea. On the west side a moat - the **Contrafossa** - was built at the same period; this separated the Old Fortress from Xopoli and meant that the fortified acropolis

rather resembled an island. Today, that moat is one of the prettiest corners in Corfu town, a peaceful anchorage where fishing-boats moor. It is spanned by an iron bridge 60 metres long, which unites the Old Fortress with the town. Where the bridge now stands, the Venetians had a wooden drawbridge, which was pulled up at night to provide even greater security.

Between the two sieges of the town by the Turks (in 1537 and 1571), major defensive works were constructed, most of them under the supervision of the engineer Sanmicheli: the Contrafossa was widened, two bastions were constructed, and in order to enhance the security of the Old Fortress the space between it and Xopoli was cleared, thus creating the **Spianada** (**Esplanade**, see p. 87, 114). The fortress itself was reinforced with additional military installations, and now only a few people dwelt inside it, though the offices of the Venetian military administration were also there. The palace of the General Proveditore were to the north, above Mandraki harbour. Nothing has now survived of this building.

p. 81

The Contrafossa or Venetian moat is today one of the most attractive places in Corfu town.

The **Venetian walls**, on three levels, have survived in very good condition together with some sections of the Byzantine fortifications and the much later works for which the British were responsible. Inside, one can see the two fine towers built by the Venetians, the **Castel del Terre**, 64 metres in height, and the **Castel de Mare**, 51 metres high, together with the ruins of gun batteries, underground tunnels, cisterns, barracks, powder magazines and other buildings dating from Venetian and British times. On the highest peak is the stone **lighthouse tower**, built in 1822 and the first lighthouse ever to guide sailors over the Greek seas. To the south is the **church of St George**, built by the British in imitation Doric style (1840).

Inside the Fortress, the Venetians erected a marble **statue** of the Austrian general **Matthias von Schulenberg**, who helped the Corfiots to repel the attempted Turkish invasion of 1716. The

p. 82

On summer evenings, the Old Fortress is an ideal spot for a romantic stroll or to enjoy the Son et Lumière show (in Greek and other languages).

p. 83

The Old Fortress as seen from the Spianada. The church of St George and, in the background, the Lighthouse can be distinguished.

statue, by the Italian sculptor A. Corrantini, has now been moved to the Spianada, outside the arched gateway to the Old Fortress.

The Old Fortress is one of the most important monuments on Corfu since it was the place where some of the most dramatic events in the island's history took place and it has been inhabited continuously for one thousand five hundred years. Apart from its historical interest, it is also one of the most attractive places on the island and forms a frequent subject for artists and photographers. From its two peaks there is a superb view of the city in one direction and the sea in the other. Sound and Light performances and dance events are held in the fortress during the summer months.

The New Fortress

After the Turkish siege of 1571, the Venetians set about implementing a fresh programme of fortificatory works, under the supervision of the engineer F. Vitelli. The basic aim was to provide protection for Xopoli, where many of the private dwellings of Venetians and Corfiots had moved. A new wall was built, sealing off the north-west side of the city, and many older structures had to be demolished to

make way for it. The west end of this new wall ended at the New Fortress, which was built between 1576 and 1588 and was later modified and supplemented by the French and the British.

The New Fortress communicated with the sea and the town through four gates. Leading south, towards the hinterland of the island, were the **Porta Raymondo** (in the direction of Garitsa) and the superb **Porta Reale** (royal gate, in the direction of Saroko). These were demolished in the nineteenth century. The two gates on the sea side have survived, however, and can still be seen, ornamented with the Lion of St Mark, emblem of Venice: they are the **Porta San Ni-**

p. 84
The New Fortress towers over the north-west part of Corfu town. In the illustration above, its north-west gate.

colo (at the north end of the Spianada) and the **Porta Spilia**, to the east of the New Fortress. These four gates communicated with the Spianada, and thus with the Old Fortress, along four roads which followed the course of the modern streets called Evgeniou Voulgari (Porta Reale), Nikiforou Theotoki (Porta Spilia), Michail Theotoki (Porta San Nicolo) and Gilfordou (Porta Raymondo).

The Venetian fortifications, seen in their day as a masterpiece of military architecture, were further supplemented in the seventeenth century by a wall to the west of the city. After the Turkish siege of 1716, the hills of Sotiros and Avrami were walled, too.

p. 85

At night, the New Fortress is floodlit, and the squares and streets beneath it, near the harbour, hum with life.

Town planning - Architecture

The nature of the urban fabric of Corfu town was dictated by the fortifications constructed by the Venetians, which occupy a large part of the ground suitable for building. Housing thus had to be kept within the walls, being confined to an area of 295,000 square metres, and the architectural form of the houses employed Venetian models adapted to the particular terrain of Corfu town.

To the east of the city, in front of the Old Fortress, is the Spianada, which in Venetian times was not an esplanade but a vast empty space, accounting for one third of the total area of the town, with a defensive role: in the event of the town being occupied, the Corfiots could take refuge in the Old Fortress and from there could fire on their attackers, who would be easy to control if they so much as approached the Spianada. The Spianada was the starting-point of the main road arteries, now called Nikiforou Theotoki and Evgeniou Voulgari Sts, which linked the Old and New Fortresses and led to the harbour further north.

Off these streets led smaller lanes and countless tiny alleys, called kantounia, producing an irregular pattern of links across the town. Many of the *kantounia*

pp. 86-87

Even today, Corfu town has preserved almost intact the atmosphere it inherited from the Venetians. The buildings and the layout of the town are reminiscent more of nearby Italy than they are of the familiar Greek architectural tradition.

were at least partially roofed, thus making it easy to move around when weather conditions were bad while at the same time providing building space since additional rooms for houses, or balconies, could be constructed over them. The main commercial streets (Nikiforou Theotoki, Evyeniou Voulgari, Michail Theotoki, Filarmonikis) were covered in this way, and their arcades (called *volta*) have survived intact down to the present day. One of the busiest commercial streets was that called the *Plati Kantouni* or Strada Larga, now named Moustoxydi St, where fairs were held and where festive events took place, especially during the Carnival season. In between these streets were numerous irregularly-shaped squares, where there would usually be a church or a well serving the surrounding houses. The districts of the town tended to take their names from the church nearest to them. Of the numerous neighbourhoods of which the three major urban districts consisted, the most densely-populated was Campiello, in the north-east part of the town. It contained the houses of many of the nobles, which stood out for their imposing architecture.

The most representative examples of Venetian architecture belonged to members of the middle and lower classes. These were

pp. 88-89

These narrow alleyways, with their old mansions, the symmetrically arched elevations of the buildings and the attractive street-lamps, are perhaps the most attractive feature of Corfu town.

usually multi-storeyed, with between three and five floors, with tiled roofs and without any sort of free space around them. The doors and windows were rectangular, or more rarely topped with round arches. Balconies were even more uncommon, but where they did exist - usually in the houses of the wealthier classes - they were notable for the delicacy of their construction. The facades of the buildings were ornamented with rows of arches, with cornices and railings at the windows, with ornamental bands to separate the storeys and with corbels. Another characteristic feature of the houses of Corfu was their chimneys, in a variety of sizes and shapes. The colours of the elevations - ochres, reds,

greens, etc. - were blended harmoniously. Of course, the most striking feature of all is the arcade (volta) on so many ground floors, which even today gives the alleys of Corfu their distinctive flavour.

The houses of the nobility were in a similar style, though they were usually lower - two or three storeys - and stood out for the care which had been taken on their construction and the money obviously spent upon it. The mansions of the rich Corfiots stood in various places all over the town, and also outside it, in the countryside. Among those which can still be seen in good condition is the Ricci mansion, in Moustoxydi St, which originally had only one storey above its arched arcade. The balcony is

pp. 90-91

Among the main features of Venetian architecture were the arcaded lower storeys - the volta - still to be seen in many Corfiot houses.

particularly fine - and is, indeed, of historical value, since it was there that the Venetian Proveditore and the Mayor of Corfu stood to watch the horse-riding competition that took place along the *Plati Kantouni* during Carnival. The **Yallinas mansion**, with an impressive arched facade, is also to be seen in the town.

The atmosphere in Corfu town today is still largely Venetian, since many of the houses which were built during that period continue to be inhabited. Buildings of the periods of French and British rule and those in the purely Greek styles of architecture combine wonderfully with these to produce fascinating aesthetic results.

p. 92
Town Hall Square, the administrative centre of Venetian Corfu.

p. 93
A street in the commercial part of town, with the bell-tower of St Spyridon in the background.

Town Hall Square (Venetian Loggia - Palace of the Latin Archbishop)

The administrative centre of the town in Venetian times lay arond the square now dominated by the Town Hall building (on Evyeniou Voulgari St). The building's foundations were laid in 1663 and construction was completed in 1691. It was originally intended as a club for the officers of the Venetian fleet, but during the greater part of later Venetian rule it was known as the **Loggia Nobilei** because it served as a kind of club for the

aristocracy. The Loggia is one of the most elegant buildings in Corfu town: it is constructed entirely in stone, in a Renaissance style, and the top floor is a later addition. On the facade, the arched doorway is flanked by four arched windows with sculptured heads at the point of the arch, and above the doorway is a niche with a bust of the Venetian admiral Francesco Morosini, in the centre of a row of ornamental reliefs.

In 1720, the Loggia was converted into a theatre, which became known as the **Theatre of San Giacomo** from the nearby Catholic church of the same name (the Catholic Cathedral, 1553). In 1733 the interior of the theatre was redesigned so that it could house performances of the opera. It remained in this form until 1902. Throughout its time as an opera house, the San Giacomo Theatre was the scene of important opera productions, and it occupied a central role in the musical education of the Corfiots. Early in the twentieth century, another storey was added to the building and since that time it has housed the municipal services of Corfu.

Also in Town Hall Square is the building which now serves as the local branch of the Bank of Greece. This was formerly the **Palace of the Latin Archbishop,** which was constructed in the early seventeenth century and later rebuilt on a number of occasions. The square was also the location of the Bailey's residence, but this has since been demolished.

pp. 94-95
Town Hall Square.
In the background,
the San Giacomo
Theatre, and on the
left the church
of St James.

CHURCH ARCHITECTURE

p. 96

The church of Our Lady 'Mandrakina'.

p. 97

The historic monastery of Our Lady 'Platytera', with its imposing bell-tower.

ost of the churches on Corfu today - and there are more than 800 of them all over the island - were built during the period of Venetian rule. Of these churches, 39 stood within the boundaries of the Venetian city, and they give us a complete picture of the church architecture of the time. The churches of Corfu belong to the 'Ionian basilica' type and the influence of the Italian Baroque on them is clear to see. Nonetheless, they tend to be plainer both outside and in terms of their interior decoration than their Italian counterparts.

Ionian basilicas are wood-roofed, single-aisled (or more rarely three-aisled) churches surrounded by an exo-narthex and notable for their monumental facades, especially in the larger churches. However, their most striking characteristic is the flat **ceiling** ornamented with paintings set in gilt frames. In most churches, the walls are covered with blue or crimson tapestries on which icons are hung. Sometimes there are wall-paintings in the exo-narthex. A carved wooden iconostasis is

also a frequent feature; this is often decorated with gilt ornaments and topped with the figure of Christ Crucified. The bell-towers are separate structures whose height means that they dominate the narrow alleys of Corfu town. They can be tower-shaped structures modelled on Italian originals, or they may be simple walls which taper towards the top where there are two or three arches from which the bells are hung.

St Spyridon

St Spyridon is the patron saint of Corfu, although he was not a Corfiot; he was born in Cyprus, and became bishop of that island. He took part in the First Ecumenical Council (held at Nicaea in Bithynia in 325 AD), and he is traditionally said to have performed his first miracle there: in order to demonstrate the indivisibility of the Holy Trinity, he dissolved a roof tile into the three elements - earth, fire and water - of which it was composed. After meeting a martyr's death in the time of Diocletian, he was canonised and his relic was kept in Constantinople, in the church of the Holy Apostles. When Constantinople fell to the Turks in 1453, the relic was bought to Corfu together with that of St Theodosia (kept in the Cathedral) and placed in an earlier church to him located in the Saroco area. When this church was demolished to make way for the Venetian walls, the island's masters, wishing to gain popularity with the Corfiots - among whom the saint's cult had begun to grow - built a new church in what is now Ayiou Spiridonos St (1589-1590). The relic of St Spyridon is kept in a silver and ebony larnax made in Venice during the nineteenth century. The larnax, in turn, is normally kept in a crypt to the right of the sanctuary.

The church of St Spyridon is a typical example of the single-aisled Ionian basilica. Next to it stands a bell-tower in the Italian style, topped with a red dome, into whose wall is built a clock. The church is very similar to the Greek church of St George in Venice. Its elevations are plain, with only a few ornamental elements.

By way of contrast, the interior is richly decorated. The ceiling was painted in the Baroque style by the local artist Panayotis Doxaras, in 1727. The ceiling is divided into 17 panels within gilt frames, which show scenes from the live of the saint, the four Evangelists, the Holy Trinity, etc. The central composition was clearly influenced by the *Apotheosis* of the Italian painter Paolo Veronese. However, only the frames of these paintings have survived from the original works: the paintings themselves, backed by

p. 98

St Spyridon.

p. 99

The Italian-style bell-tower of St Spyridon is one of the most prominent features in the centre of Corfu town.

cloth, were ruined by damp. The paintings we see today are mid-nineteenth century work, superimposed on the originals by N. Aspiotis. In the narthex are four interesting icons by the Corfiot painter S. Sperantzas, while the icons on the iconostasis are the work of Spyros Prosalentis, another local artist. The iconostasis itself is marble, made by the architect M. Mauers (nineteenth century). Inside the church is a vast collection of votive offerings, the largest of which were dedicated by the rich families of Corfu. A special place among them belongs to the two large silver lamps dedicated by the General Providetore of the Sea after the successful conclusion of the siege of 1716.

St Spyridon and the history of this island are one and the same thing: "*The island is really the Saint: and the Saint is the island. Nearly all the male children are named after him. All the island craft carry his tintype - mournful of bed and brow - nailed to their masts of unseasoned cypress wood*". (Lawrence Duhrell Prospero's Cell, Penguin, London 1978). According to the local tradition, it was St Spyridon who saved the islanders during the Turkish siege of 1716: on 11 August of that year, he appeared bearing a lighted torch, and the island's foes turned and fled. Each year on that day, the Corfiots hold a procession in commemoration of their saviour. The relic of the saint is also carried in procession on 12 December, St Spyridon's day, on the first Sunday in November and on

Palm Sunday (to commemorate the saint's miraculous intervention to save the island from outbreaks of plague in 1629 and 1673), and on Easter Saturday (to mark yet another occasion, during the sixteenth century, when St Spyridon saved the island from epidemic). All these processions were established as far back as Venetian times.

The Cathedral (Our Lady 'Spiliotissa'):

The Orthodox Cathedral of Corfu was built in 1577 near the New Fortress and the harbour, on a site previously occupied by a church of St Blaise. It was dedicated to Our Lady 'Spiliotissa' during the period of British rule, since an icon of Our Lady by that name was moved there from another church demolished at that time. Today, the church houses the relic of St Theodosia, who is commemorated in the church on 11 February along with St Blaise. However, the church's most important festival is that of 15 August, the day dedicated to the Dormition of Our Lady.

The Cathedral is a three-aisled basilica with a most impressive facade modelled on Renaissance originals. Inside, there is an elegant Byzantine iconostasis, together with quite a number of icons by important painters. The earliest of these is that called *Our Lady of Demosiana*, and it is a double-sided icon showing Our Lady 'Hodeghetria' on one side and St St Arsenius on the other. It must have

been painted in Ioannina in the late fourteenth century. Among the other icons, the most interesting are those of *St George and the Dragon*, by Michail Damaskinos (sixteenth century), *St Gobdelas*, by Emmanouil Tzanes Bounialis (seventeenth century, on the iconostasis), and the *Last Supper*, by Panayotis Paramythiotis (eighteenth century).

Our Lady 'Antivouniotissa':,

or, Our Lady the All-Holy Mother of God (in the Campiello district of town, on a street with steps running at right angles to Arseniou St). This church was built in the second half of the fifteenth century, as a basilica with an exo-narthex

around three sides. The church belonged to four of the richest families on Corfu and its exo-narthex contains the tombs of many noblemen, as can be seen from the coats-of-arms on their tombs. The ceiling of the church is of particular interest: it consists not of paintings on a backing of canvas, as is usually the case in the churches of Corfu, but of wood-carvings with gilt motifs. In the exo-narthex are traces of wall-paintings, and an important collection of post-Byzantine icons has been on display in the nave since 1994. The collection includes the *St Justine and Sts Sergius and Bacchus* by Michail Damaskinos (1571), *St Cyril of*

p. 101
The cathedral church of Our Lady 'Spilaiotissa', with the striking marble door of its main elevation.

Alexandria and *Nole me Tangere* by Emmanouil Tzanes Bounialis (1654, 1657), *Our Lady Hodeghetria* and *Christ Pantocrator* (1629) by Emmanouil Lombardos, *The Invention and Exaltation of the Holy Cross* by Emmanouil Skordilis (1650-1675), the *In Thee Rejoices* by Ioannis Moschos (late seventeenth century), and *St Alexius* by Stefanos Tzankarolas (late seventeenth century).

p. 102

The Italian-style bell-tower of Our Lady of Tenedos.

Our Lady 'Kremasti':

This church stands in one of the prettiest Corfiot squares (close to Komninon St), where there is an attractive sixteenth-century well. According to one view, the church took its name (which means 'hanging') from an icon of Our Lady which hung on the wall rather than being placed on the iconostasis, as was more usual. The church dates from the sixteenth

century and is a single-aisled basilica with an exo-narthex along three of its sides. Of this exo-narthex, only the west part has remained, and the ceiling paintings inside the church have also been destroyed. There is an impressive stone iconostasis in front of the sanctuary, and the church also contains large-scale icons in the Western style by Spyros Sperantzas (eghteenth century).

St Nicholas 'ton Geronton'

(in the Campiello district):
This church was built in the early sixteenth century and is a single-aisled basilica with an exo-narthex. It was the Cathedral church of the 'Great High Priests' when that institution was operative. The most interesting features of the church are the ambo on the north wall and the elaborate iconostasis in front of the sanctuary. On the doors in the

p. 103

A view of Our Lady 'Kremasti', behind an attractive sixteenth-century Italian well.

iconostasis are paintings of *St Theodora, St Cercyra* and *Communion of the Apostles*, all of which may have been created by Emmanouil Bounialis in the seventeenth century.

Pantocrator: The church of Christ Pantocratos was flattened by German bombing in 1944 and has now been reconstructed. It was built in the second half of the sixteenth century, in the Campiello quarter, and it is a single-aisled basilica. Some iconostasis icons of the seventeenth century by Emmanouil Tzanes Bounialis originated in this church, but the iconostasis to be seen today dates from the eighteenth century and has icons by Georgios Chrysoloras.

Our Lady 'ton Xenon': This church is in Ipeirou St and it belonged to the people of Epirus who took refuge in Corfu during the period of Ottoman rule. It is a three-aisled basilica with a ceiling painted in the eighteenth century by N. Koutouzis. Inside, the visitor is impressed by the vast number of votive offerings brought by the Epirot founders from their homeland.

St John the Baptist: Near Our Lady 'ton Xenon' is St John, a single-aisled basilica with an exo-narthex (sixteenth century), in which Nikiforos Theotokis was once priest. The marble iconostasis with icons by Georgios Chrysoloras has survived.

Platytera Monastery: In Ioulia Andreadi St, outside the boundaries of the Venetian town, is the Playtera Monastery, built in the eighteenth century and demolished by the French in 1799. The foundation was soon rebuilt, and later became the place where Ioannis Capodistrias and the Corfiot historian Andreas Moustoxydis were buried. Inside the church are superb post-Byzantine icons: the *Revelation* of Theodoros Poulakis, the *Virgin and Child* of Emmanouil Tzanes Bounialis, the *Second Coming* of Georgios Klontzas, two paintings by N. Kantounis (eighteenth century), and iconostasis icons by N. Koutouzis (eighteenth century).

Our Lady of Tenedos: This church, close to the New Fortress, took its name from the island of Tenedos, refugees from which took shelter on Corfu during the Ottoman period. The church is notable for its marked Baroque style and is also of historical interest, since the first printing-press on Corfu once operated in its nave.

Among the other churches of the Venetian period, the most notable are San Giacomo (the Catholic Cathedral, 1553) in Town Hall Square, Our Lady of Mandraki (1700, by the Old Fortress), St Antony (fourteenth century, the oldest church in the town), and the Holy Trinity (early seventeenth century).

p. 104
'Christ as the Great High Priest', by Emmanouil Lombardos (1629).

Religious painting (Cretan School - Ionian school)

p. 106

'Our Lady Hodeghetria', an icon by Michail Damaskinos (sixteenth century).

p. 107

'Noli me tangere', an icon by Emmanouil Tzanes (late sixteenth - early seventeenth century).

The geographical position of Corfu close to the West, the many centuries of Christian domination, and the desire of the Venetians to overcome demographic difficulties by encouraging the settlement of immigrants on the island were the fundamental reasons why Greeks from the Turkish-occupied parts of the country tended to move to Corfu. At a very early date, groups of migrants from Crete arrived, and this trickle swelled to a flood during the Cretan War of 1645-1669 and after the fall of Handak (Herakleio) and all Crete to the Turks in 1669. Among the migrants were many prominent families together with priests, scholars, icon-painters and craftsmen, who grafted their culture on to that of the Ionian islands. They brought with them whatever they managed to salvage from the ruin of their homeland and keep through the difficult conditions of the journey: religious treasures, pieces of jewellery, wood carvings, books, sacred vessels and icons. These icons ornamented many of the churches of Corfu and are still there today, providing scholars of the religious painting of the era with invaluable material to study. Most of the icons date from the late sixteenth, seventeenth and eighteenth centuries, and were produced by what is called the Cretan school of painting. The artists who managed to make their way to the Ionian islands continued their careers there, coming under the influences of their new homeland and of nearby Italy. In a reciprocal manner, a local artistic tradition grew up under their influence, leading to the appearance of what is called the Ionian school of painting.

The **Cretan school of painting** developed in Crete between the fifteenth century and the fall of the island to the Turks in 1669. The Cre-

tan painters of the fifteenth century followed the trends in late Palaeologan icon-painting, the principal characteristics of which were rhythm of composition, plasticity in the masses, heavily marked outlines, schematic folds in the garments, gentle movement and serenity in the figures. In some cases, the technique and iconography were enhanced by borrowings from fourteenth-century Italian art. Very few icons of this period have survived in Corfu, although one icon by the famous painter **Angelos** is an exception. During the last thirty years of the sixteenth century, two Cretan painters, Michail Damaskinos (1530-1592) and Georgios Klontzas (1562-1608), set their seal on the island's painting. Under the influence of Italian Mannerism, they revitalised the expressive media of the Cretan school. One important work by **Georgios Klontzas**, the *Second Coming*, can be seen in Platytera Monastery. Influenced by the work of Michelangelo under the same title, this icon is a small-scale composition with a wealth of figures rendered in strict symmetry and vivid colours. Corfu can also boast the largest known group of signed works by **Michail Damaskinos** of Herakleio, who worked on the island for approximately two years (1582-?1584). Some of his works display fidelity to the Byzantine approach, while in others we can discern some penetration of Italian elements. In a third group, these features are much more strikingly present. The innovations of Michail Damaskinos had repercussions throughout the post-Byzantine painting of the seventeenth century.

In the early seventeenth century, however, painters returned to the models of the fifteenth century and rarely made use of the developments that had come about in Italian art. A leading figure at this time was **Emmanouil Lombardos**, five of whose icons, notable for their

p. 108
. The Hospitality of Abraham', an icon from the Antivouniotissa Museum (late sixteenth or early seventeenth century).

skilful technique and linear moulding of form, are in Corfu. Also at this period, the Corfiot painter **Emmanouil Tzanfournaris**, who was of Cretan descent, spent most of his career working in Venice (1595-1631).

Two of the most important Greek icon-painters of the late seventeenth century lived in Corfu and left an indelible mark on developments in their field of art: **Emmanouil Tzanes Bounialis** (1610-1690) and **Theodoros Poulakis** (†1692). Emmanouil Tzanes Bounialis, a priest from Rethymno in Crete, left his native island in 1648 and spent some ten years in Corfu. Apart from his artistic achievements, Bounialis was also a composer of religious music. Another of Bounialis' innovations was the replacement of the low doors in the iconostasis (which separates the sanctuary from the nave) with doors made from a single leaf. These doors were first used in the church of Sts Jason and Sosipater, for which Tzanes painted at least six icons. Many of these introduced new iconographic types for depicting St Cyril of Alexandria (showing the saint wearing a dalmatic and a mitre rather than the traditional chasuble) and St John Damascene, who was now painted in priestly robes rather than a monk's habit and a turban. The work of Tzanes is notable for the precision of its technique and the painter's firmness in applying the rules of the Cretan tradition of much earlier times. In many of his icons, we can detect a more extensive Italian influence, which reflected the spirit of the early Classical Renaissance.

Theodoros Poulakis died in Corfu in 1692 and was buried in the church of St Spyridon. Most of his works, which stand out for their skilful rendering of detail, were influenced by the Flemish school of engraving, whose techniques he was able to handle with notable success. One interesting icon,

p. 109
'St Alexius' an icon by Stefanos Tzankarolas from the Antivouniotissa Museum (late seventeenth century).

which has survived in the church of Our Lady at Kassiopi, shows *The Virgin and Child and the Miracle of Our Lady of Kassiopi*. It was dedicated to commemorate the fact that the painter had survived a terrible storm while sailing from Corfu to Venice in 1671.

Tzanes and Poulakis were not the only painters working in Corfu at this time: the others included **Victor** (1651-1697) and **Filotheos Skoufos**, who represented the traditional approach to icon-painting and the techniques of earlier times, repeating the models they had learned from their own teachers.

After the fall of Crete in 1669, the tradition of the Cretan school was kept up by a new generation of emigrant painters who set up studios here and there in the Ionian islands and took on local pupils. The artists of the Ionian islands thus continued the Cretan tradition, which they enhanced with elements from the Italian technique, now accepted in the islands. These new trends led to the emergence of what is called Ionian painting, the production of which centred on Corfu and Zakynthos. However, **Ionian painting** is nothing more or less than the natural continuation of the Cretan school as experienced by the artists who learned it in the studios of the Ionian islands. At this time, the most important painters of Corfu were **Stefanos Tzankarolas**, famed for the accuracy of his drawing, and **Constantinos Kontarinis** (early eighteenth century), both of whom followed

the lead of Emmanouil Tzanes.

The most important representative of the Ionian school, and its theoretician, was **Panayotis Doxaras** (1662-1729), who was born in the Mani (southern Peloponnese). In his ceiling paintings for the church of St Spyridon (1727), Doxaras introduced Italian art into the churches of the Ionian islands. In 1726, his *Concerning Painting*, written in Corfu, laid the theoretical foundations for the new trends in painting and put forward the great masters of the Italian Renaissance as models to be imitated. The successors of Panayotis Doxaras, his son **Nikolaos Doxaras**, **Nikolaos Kantounis** (1768-1834), and **Nikolaos Koutouzis** (1741-1813), finalised the form of Ionian art and made it into the starting-point for secular modern Greek painting as it was to develop during the nineteenth century (see 'Intellectual and Artistic Life, Nineteenth and Twentieth Century').

Intellectual life

Under Venetian rule, the process of organising education does not seem to have been fostered in the Ionian islands. Opportunities for education were not often available for the lower classes - especially those who worked the land - though it was possible for the wealthier town-dwellers to study in Italy, especially at the University of Padua. The first literary society of Corfu, called the Academy of the

Assured ('Accademia degli Assicurati'), was set up in 1656, and it was followed by the Academy of the Productive ('Accademia dei Fertili'). A third academy, of the Wanderers ('Quos Phoebus Vocat Errantes') was founded in 1732, but its impact seems to have been slight.

Although the intellectual life of Corfu itself was limited, quite a number of Corfiots were active in the dissemination of Greek learning abroad. **Antonios Eparchos**, one of the Greeks who dealt in manuscripts in Venice, was a Corfiot. He took refuge in Venice after the siege of 1537, founding schools and selling manuscripts - many of which he had copied himself - from his own library. Another Corfiot, **Matthaios Devaris**, worked during the same period on the compilation of catalogues of the manuscripts in the Vatican Library. The Corfiot literary scholar **Nikolaos Sofianos**, who prepared the first grammar of the Greek vernacular (spoken) language, in the sixteenth century, wrote codices and was a printer and cartographer. Two of the most important scholars among those conventionally known as Teachers of the Nation - Nikiforos Theotokis and Evyenios Voulgaris - were from Corfu. **Nikiforos Theotokis** (1731-1800), belonged to an eminent Corfiot family and studied medicine and science in Bologna and Padua. In 1775, he became director of the 'Authentic Academy' at Jassy in Romania, and in 1779 he was ordained as Archbishop of Slavonia and Cherson. In 1792, he retired to the Monastery of St Daniel in Moscow, where he died eight years later. **Evyenios Voulgaris** (1716-1806) began his studies in Arta and later studied divinity, philosophy, ancient Greek, Latin, Hebrew literature, languages and science at Patavia in Italy. In 1737, he became a monk and in 1753 he took over as director of the Athonias School; here, however, his progressive views brought him into conflict with the conservative establishment of the Athonite religious community and in 1759 he retired into a monastery on Mt Athos. Later, he taught at the Patriarchal School in Constantinople (1753), and in 1763 he became a publisher's editor in Leipzig. In this capacity, he met Catherine the Great of Russia, who appointed him librarian to, and a member of, the Academy of Petersburg. Ordination as Archbishop of Slavonia and Cherson followed, in 1775, and after eleven years in this post Voulgaris retired to the Monastery of St Alexander Nevsky in Petersburg, where he died. Voulgaris was known for his breadth of spirit and his profound knowledge in many fields. He wrote many treatises of the greatest value and translated numerous works of antiquity (including the *Aeneid* and the *Georgics* of Virgil) into modern Greek. Both Voulgaris and Nikiforos Theotokis worked systematically to disseminate Greek learning outside the narrow confines of their homeland, and they occupy positions of honour in the history of Greek intellectual affairs.

4. CORFU IN THE NINETEENTH CENTURY

p. 112

View of Corfu town, with the Palace of St Michael and St George.

p. 113

The Liston building, with its elegant arches, on the north-west side of the Spianada.

Neither the French nor the British made substantive changes to the fabric that had developed in the town of Corfu under Venetian rule. The new buildings they constructed blended into the architectural style that had already taken shape, and in fact it is often difficult to tell them apart from earlier structures. The French concentrated on improving the appearance of the town, and were the first to lay the Spianada out as a public square. The British were more interested in town planning, introducing building regulations and taking measures to safeguard public health and supply the buildings with water. Under British rule, the fortifications of Corfu were strengthened and new structures were added to both the Old and the New Fortress. Interesting public buildings were also constructed, public works were carried out, and charitable institutions were founded; most of these were the result of initiatives by High Commissioner Douglas. In his honour, a marble monument usually known as **the obelisk of Douglas** (1843) was set up at Garitsa, at the intersection of Alexandras and Dimokratias Sts. On the base of the monument an inscription in Greek refers to the Commissioner's achievements, and there are also reliefs executed by the Corfiot sculptor Ioannis-Vaptistis Kalosgouros (1794-1878).

The Spianada

The Spianada is one of the largest public squares in the Balkans. The Venetians created it in the period from 1537 to 1571 as an open space in front of the Old Fortress where the inhabitants could defend themselves more effectively in the event of an attack on the city. Under the French, the area was planted with trees and landscaped as an esplanade. Since that time, it has been the centre of Corfu town and most of the collective activities of the towns people still take place there.

The north-west side of the square is occupied by the imposing row of buildings called the **Liston**, an elegant arcaded structure ornamented with elaborate lanterns. It was built in 1807-1814 by the French engineer M. Lesseps (father of the builder of the Suez Canal), and it imitates the arcades of the rue de Rivoli in Paris. Today, the arcade houses the most refined of the cafes of Corfu town and some of the island's best restaurants.

In 1816, the engineer J. Whitemore built the **Maitland Monument** on the south-east side of the Spianada. This circular, neo-Classical structure consists of Ionic columns supporting a superstructure ornamented with floral motifs in relief. Above its architrave is an inscription noting the dedication to Thomas Maitland, first British High Commissioner. Under the British, this was the entrance to the underground water tanks from which Corfu town was supplied, for which reason it is also known as 'the Cistern'.

The Ionian Academy

In Akadimias St, at the south end of the Spianada, stands the building which housed the famous Ionian Academy. This was in effect the first Greek university, and it was founded in 1824 by Lord F.N. Guildford, the British Philhellene, who was in charge of public education in the Ionian Islands. Before the time of the Ionian Academy, and dating back to French rule, efforts had been made to foster the development of education

pp. 114-115

The Spianada is the largest city square in Greece and the social life of Corfu focuses on it. In the background, the New Fortress and the harbour.

in Corfu. In 1808, Ioannis Capodistrias had played a leading role in the founding of an educational institution which was also called the Ionian Academy and whose purpose was to develop the arts and sciences and refine agriculture. This Academy, which possessed a library and a botanical garden, had 28 full members and offered courses in physics, economics and politics, taught in Italian. Greek was recognised as the official language of the Academy in 1817 and was also used as the teaching medium when the Ionian Academy was refounded by Guildford in 1824. This new university, whose emblem was the owl, consisted of four Facul-

ties: of Divinity, Arts, Law and Medicine. Among the important local personalities who worked on the teaching staff were the historian and literary scholar Andreas Moustoxydis, Petros Vrailas Armenis (Foreign Minister of Greece after unification), and the poet Andreas Calvos of Zakynthos. The Ionian Academy functioned down to the time of union with Greece, after which the national educational system was organised around the University of Athens. The Ionian Academy building was almost completely destroyed by German bombing in 1943.

Today, a **statue of Lord Guildford** stands in the Municipal Gardens of Corfu, on the north-east side of the Spianada. The statue is the work of the sculptor K. Apergis and it shows the founder of the Academy with an open book in his hand. Very close to this is another important work, a bust of the poet Lorentzos Mavilis.

The Palace of Sts Michael and George

The Palace of Sts Michael and George occupies the north side of the Spianada, where under the French (1807-1814) there was an enormous military hospital. The construction of the palace was the initiative of High Commissioner Thomas Maitland, and it was used as his official residence, as the seat of the Ionian Senate and Treasury, and as the headquarters of the Order of St Michael and St George, from which it took its name. The Order was founded in England in 1818 for the purpose of awarding medals to residents of Malta and the Ionian Islands who had per-

pp. 116-117

The Palace of St Michael and St George with the statue of Frederick Adam.

formed important services for Great Britain.

The Palace was built between 1819 and 1824 to plans by the architect J. Whitemore. It consists entirely of Maltese stone, in the British version of the neo-Classical order. The main building has three storeys and is linked by two arches - that of St Michael to the east and that of St George to the west - to two semicircular wings. On the facade are 32 Doric columns - replicas of those on the Parthenon - and ornamentation with symbolic reliefs depicting the Ionian islands. They were the work of the Maltese sculptor Dimech and the Corfiot artist P. Prosalentis. A statue representing Great Britain was originally located above these reliefs, but was removed by the British when they withdrew in 1864 and replaced by a sculpture depicting the prow of a Corfiot trireme.

The entrance portico leads through doors into an antechamber laid out on three levels and ornamented with Ionic columns and friezes showing scenes from the *Odyssey*. The two side doors gave access to the Parliament hall (moved in 1855 to another building) and to the Senate, where the original furniture is still in place, with busts of the Speakers and portraits of Commissioners Maitland and Adam and of King George IV of Britain. From the ground floor antechamber a magnificent staircase leads to the antechamber on the first floor, supported on Corinthian columns. Here are the three sumptuous reception rooms: the circular ballroom, the throne-room and the banqueting hall. The original throne of the High Commissioners is still in the throne-room, together with paintings presenting St Michael and St George. The paintings of King George IV and King George I of Greece are copies of the originals. The private apartments of the British High Commissioners are in the wings to the east and west.

In 1837, gardens and baths were added to the Palace. In the same year, a **bronze statue** of High Commissioner **Frederick Adam** (1824-1832) was placed in the centre garden, to commemorate the construction, on his initiative, of the Corfu aqueduct and of various other public works. The statue was the work of the sculptor P. Prosalentis and it shows Adam, dressed in a Roman toga, pointing to a small tank containing water at the foot of the statue.

In 1864, after unification, the Palace was used as the summer residence of the Greek royal family. After the Second World War, most of the building was made over to the Ministry of Education, to house the archives of the Ionian Academy, the Archaeological Service, the Public Library (60,000 volumes), a Byzantine collection (see p. 77), and a valuable collection of Asiatic art.

Museum of Asiatic Art

The **Museum of Asiatic Art** is housed in the two wings which once contained the private apartments of the High Commissioner. In was founded in 1927 (as the Museum of Sino-Japanese art) and consists of more than 11,000 art-works originally belonging to various private and state collections. Its nucleus was the G. Manos collection, with more than 10,000 works of Chinese and Japanese art, which was donated to the Greek State in 1919.

Gallery A contains Chinese exhibits from the Shang (1500-1027 BC), Chou (1027-221 BC), Han (221 BC-220 AD), Vei (386-534 AD), T'ang (618-907) and Sung (960-1297) dynasties: pottery, bronze vessels, funerary statuettes, Buddhist statues and priceless porcelain vases.

In *Gallery B* are art-works of the Ming dynasty (1368-1644), dating from the time when Chinese art was at its zenith: bronze vases, figurines, enamels, porcelain, paintings, wood-carvings, seals and coins.

Gallery C is given over to the first phase in the Ch'ing dynasty (1662-1722): porcelain, figurines, seals and other items made from sem-precious stones.

The second phase of this dynasty is covered by *Gallery D*: porcelain, jewellery, sceptres, paintings and small vases.

Gallery E contains garments, lengths of material and pieces of furniture from the Ch'ing dynasty.

Gallery F focuses on art-works from Japan: Neolithic tools and weapons of the period from the second century BC to the third century AD, copies of funerary statuary from the third to the sixth century AD, wood-carvings, paintings and pottery of the fourteenth-eighteenth centuries AD.

Gallery G presents the kind of weapons used by the Samurai (sixteenth-eighteenth century), masks from the Noh theatre (1338-1578), and two paintings showing scenes from the Kabuki theatre and Samurai warriors.

In *Gallery H* (the ballroom) are works of Japanese miniature craftsmanship from the Endo period (1615-1868).

Gallery I (the banqueting-hall) is also devoted to this period: it contains pottery, musical instru-

p. 119
Funerary figurine of a dancer, in terracotta;
T'ang dynasty (618-907 AD).

ments, miniatures and wood carvings.

Gallery J has a collection of figurines from India and Japan, together with Japanese screens.

Works of art from Thibet, Nepal and Pakistan can be seen in *Gallery K*. Note, in particular, the Buddhist sculptures from Ghandara, now a province of Pakistan, in which elements of Hellenistic art - imported during the campaigns of Alexander the Great in the area - can be clearly seen.

Gallery L contains works of art from India, covering the period from the early Christian era to the nineteenth century.

Gallery M has a collection of wood carvings from India (eighteenth-nineteenth century), with sculptures from Cambodia and Siam and interesting painted screens from Korea.

The Literary Association

To the north-west of the Spianada is the building of the Corfu Literary Association, one of the oldest learned societies in Greece. It was founded in 1836 by the Corfiot philosopher and diplomat Petros Vrailas Armenis, and it was used as a library and reading-room. Today it still has an interesting library of books on the Ionian islands, manuscripts, engravings, paintings and icons. Exhibitions and lectures are often held in the building.

The Ionian Parliament

At the end of Moustoxydi St is the building of the Ionian Parliament, designed in 1855 by the Corfiot architect I. Chronis. On 23 September 1863, it was in this chamber that the union of the

p. 120

Bronze tea vessel with cloisonné enamelling; Ming dynasty (1368-1644).

p. 121

The Literary Association building, to the north-west of the Spianada.

Ionian islands with Greece was proclaimed. Two plaques built into the facade commemorate Union and, with 12 Doric columns, are all that survive of the original structure: the remainder was flattened by German bombing in 1943 and later rebuilt. Today, the interior houses the **Museum of the Fighters for the Freedom of the Ionian Islands,** containing portraits of the Speakers of the Ionian Parliament (1848-1864), manuscripts, and other items connected with the struggles of the people of the Ionian islands for union with Greece.

The Old Prefecture Building

The Old Prefecture building, to the north of the Spianada, was built in the mid-nineteenth century by the architect I. Chronis and in the time of the Ionian state was the residence of the Speaker of Parliament. It is one of the most important examples of the architecture of the British period. As we are told by a plaque on the facade, an earlier house which stood on the same site was the birthplace of Ioannis Capodistrias. The building now houses the Department of Translation and Interpreting of the Ionian University.

pp. 122-123
The Old Prefecture building to the north of the Spianada, on the site once occupied by the Capodistrias house.

Ioannis Capodistrias

Ioannis Capodistrias, the first Governor of free Greece, was born in Corfu in 1776 to an aristocratic family whose name appeared in the *Libro d'Oro*. From 1794 to 1797 he studied Latin in Venice and medicine in Padua, after which he returned to Corfu and practised as a doctor. In 1801, the Ionian Senate assigned him the task of imple-

menting the first Constitution of the Septinsular Republic, appointing him as Secretary to the Republic in 1803 and chairman of the committee compiling the new Constitution in 1806. This new Constitution was described as the most democratic of its time, since the principal criterion for participation in public affairs was no longer the aristocratic origin of the citizens but the level of their income. It was on the initiative of Capodistrias that the first Ionian Academy was founded in 1808 and that education was extended so as to be available to the lower social classes.

During the second period of French rule, Capodistrias moved to Russia - on the invitation of Tsar Alexander - and was appointed to the Russian Foreign Ministry, serving in the Embassy in Vienna and on the diplomatic staff of General Chichagov in

Bucharest (1808-1811). Among his particular successes was his participation in the process of drawing up the first constitution of Switzerland (1813-1814), and he attended all the European Congresses held after 1816. As early as 1815, the Tsar had formally appointed him Russian Foreign Minister. In that post, Capodistrias fought the diplomatic battle for the rights of the peoples against absolutist regimes, with the ultimate aim of preparing the ground for the liberation of Greece. As part of that endeavour, he gave many Greeks the opportunity to study at European universities, provided financial support for Greek communities in the European countries, and contributed to the founding of schools and churches in order to maintain the Greek identity intact outside Greece as well as in it. In addition, he brought powerful arguments to bear on the Great Powers in favour of the unification of Europe, with the equal participation of the smaller countries. Capodistrias also did much to help end the slave trade.

In 1819, he visited Corfu and then travelled on to London, where he submitted protests over the illiberal regime by which the British were governing Corfu. In 1820-1821, his presence at the Congresses of Tropau and Leibach was of decisive importance: Europe, which was determined to crush the revolts that had broken out in Spain and Italy,

resolved to follow the same policy towards the Greek War of Independence, which had broken out in the meantime. Capodistrias succeeded in demonstrating that the Greek War of Independence was quite a different matter (since it was being waged against foreign conquerors who were members of a different religion) and in preventing the sending of troops to Greece to help the Turks suppress the revolution. And in 1822, when the Tsar refused to send troops to fight on the Greek side, Capodistrias resigned from his diplomatic corps - though his resignation was not accepted. In 1822-1827, he settled in Geneva and fought to strengthen the current of public opinion in favour of a free Greece.

Capodistrias finally resigned from his Russian posts in 1827 and moved to Greece, where the Third National Assembly had elected him Governor of the country. In 1828, he arrived in Nafplio and immediately travelled on to Aigina, which was then capital of the emergent Greek state. When the capital was moved to Nafplio in 1830, he established the headquarters of his government there and stayed in the town until his death in 1831, with the exception of brief trips to Poros. During the four years or so in which Capodistrias ruled the fledgling Greek state, his style of government was seen as pioneering for its time. Although the state he took over was in a state of ruin, he succeeded in organising most of its sectors on the basis of liberal ideas. His main contribution was in the fields of social welfare and education: hospitals were set up to provide treatment for all the classes of society, orphanages were opened to care for the victims of war, land was distributed to the peasants, teachers were trained, ecclesiastical, farming and technical schools were established, and institutions such as the university, the national library and the national archaeological museum were founded. Capodistrias also made much progress on the compilation of the body of laws which the new state would need, on founding a bank, on setting up military cadet schools and army camps, on suppressing the piracy that was the scourge of the Greek seas, and on organising a proper navy.

However, his firm policy of defending the rights of the lower social classes soon brought him into conflict with the local magnates and ship-owners, whose interests were directly affected by such an approach. Furthermore, his refusal to contemplate any form of foreign intervention created an atmosphere of displeasure abroad with the political line he was following. As a result, his rivals managed to have him assassinated on 27 September 1827, just as he entered the church of St Spyridon in Nafplio. The murder of Capodistrias has been acknowledged by scholars as one of the events that changed the course of modern Greek history.

The tomb of Ioannis Capodistrias is at Platytera Monastery in Corfu town. His summer residence, in the village of Evropouli, is now a museum. His **statue** stands in Corfu town, opposite the Ionian Academy; the Governor is depicted standing, wrapped in his cloak, with a thoughtful expression.

Intellectual and artistic life (nineteenth and twentieth centuries)

The arrival of the French in Corfu, in 1797, marked the beginning of the development of the intellectual life of the island. During the first period of French rule, a **department of state education** was set up, together with a **library**, and the first **printing house** in Greece opened as a department of the administration which printed government material. During the second period of French rule, the **Ionian Academy** was founded; it was reorganised under the British and survived down to the time of unification with Greece in 1864 (see p. 115).

The teaching staff of the Ionian Academy included the important Corfiot historian and scholar **Andreas Moutsoxydis** (1785-1860). Moutsoxydis, who held a doctorate from the University of Patavia, was appointed historiographer to the Septinsular Republic in 1806 and until the end of his life conducted research into the history of the island and published papers, newspapers (*Ellinikos Tachydromos*) and periodicals (*Ellinomnimon*). He also studied the literature of ancient Greece, and under the administration of Ioannis Capodistrias undertook the task of organising the educational institutions of Aigina. After the death of Capodistrias, he became a Senator in Corfu and Director of the island's educational system.

The intellectual life of Corfu flourished as never before during the period in which the Greek national poet, **Dionysios Solomos**, lived there (from 1828 to 1857). Solomos (1798-1857) was born in Zakynthos, where he began his education, conducted in Italian. After successful studies in Italy and making the acquaintance of leading scholars and poets of his age, he returned to Zakynthos in 1818 and threw himself into the linguistic controversy which at that time had divided men of letters into two camps. Solomos himself was in favour of the use of the vernacular (spoken) language, and opposed those who believed that the principal instrument for enlightening the people ought to be the ancient Greek tongue, which had long ceased to be in use by ordinary folk. Of course, Solomos' first poems were written in Italian; he only began to use Greek

after 1822. The War of Independence and the struggle to throw off the Ottoman yoke struck deep into the soul of the poet, who in 1824, in just a month, wrote the 158 verses of his famous *Hymn to Liberty*. The poem was set to music by the Corfiot composer Nikolaos Mantzaros and established itself as the national anthem of Greece. In 1828, Solomos moved to Corfu, which as capital of the Ionian state could provide him with the intellectual stimulation he required. The period during which he lived in Corfu proved to be the most fruitful of his life, and during it he produced poetry of the highest quality: *Lambros, The Woman of Zakynthos, and* his masterpiece, *The Free Besieged,* on the subject of the siege of Mesolonghi by the Turks in 1825-1826.

By blending Romanticism and the Classical spirit, Solomos played a most important part in the evolution of modern Greek literature. His statue stands in Armeniou St today, outside the house where the poet lived and died, which since 1964 has been the **Solomos Museum**. It contains portraits, busts, photographs, manuscripts, letters, and an exhibition of the poet's books and personal effects.

During his Corfu period, Solomos was the centre of a large circle of men of letters and authors, and his work had a considerable impact on the literature of his time. After his death, Solomos' pupils formed an independent 'school' in Greek literature, known as the Ionian school. Among its members, the most important for the intellectual history of Corfu was **Iakovos Polylas** (1826-1898), who was a friend of Solomos and in 1859 published his manuscripts. Polylas also wrote valuable critical papers and commentaries on Solomos. He distinguished himself as a translator into modern Greek of Homer's *Odyssey* and *Iliad*, of Tyrtaeus, of Shakespeare and of Goethe, and he wrote poems and short stories of his own. He was also a political figure, serving as a representative of Corfu in the Greek Parliament and publishing newspapers which carried articles by him (*Anayennisi, Rigas Ferraios* and others). Another member of the Ionian school was **Gerasimos Markoras** (1826-1911), who was influenced both by Solomos and by the Parnassian movement and concerned himself primarily with the concepts of patriotism, death and love.

Among the distinctive figures of the next generation of poets was **Lorentzos Mavilis** (1860-1912 author of many fine sonnets), who acquired an extensive education in Corfu, Athens and Germany and who came under the

p. 127
View of the
Solomos Museum
in Corfu town.

influence of Kant and Indian philosophy. He translated the Latin classics into Greek and German and established the sonnet as a verse-form in Greek. Mavilis was noted for his nobility of character and for his love of his homeland, which he demonstrated in practice by fighting against the Turks in Crete in 1896-1897 and, ultimately, by giving his life for his country during the struggle to liberate Epirus during the First Balkan War of 1912-1913. Among his close friends was **Constantinos Theotokis** (1872-1923), from Karousades in Corfu, an important prose-writer who took his themes primarily from rural life.

The predominant figure in the musical world of Corfu was **Nikolaos Mantzaros** (1795-1872), the composer who in 1864 wrote the music to Solomos' patriotic poem *Hymn to Liberty*, which became the Greek national anthem. However, Mantzaros' contribution to music in Corfu did not stop there: he founded the Old Corfu Philharmonic in 1840, and was principally respon-

p. 128
Dionysios Solomos
(1798-1857).

sible for the gigantic steps forward made by music on the island. He took the initiative that led to the formation of a group of important musicians (S. Xyndas, A. Liveralis and others) who composed operas and were more than capable of forming the orchestra at the San Giacomo Theatre where the operas were performed. In 1890, a second Philharmonic (brass band) was founded on the island and given the name 'Mantzaros' in honour of the composer. The foundations for the development of the fine arts in Corfu were laid by the establishment of an art school on the island as far back as 1810. The founder, and principal teacher, of the school was **Pavlos Prosalentis** (1784-1837), who had studied architecture, sculpture, literature and economics in Rome. As a student of the Italian sculptor Antonio Canova, Prosalentis' works expressed the ideas of neo-Classicism, and he became the official sculptor of the Septinsular Republic. In 1815, the British recognised Prosalentis' achievements by making his school a public institution. Today, his work is seen as being of fundamental importance for sculpture not only in the Ionian islands but throughout Greece in general. He was assisted by two other important sculptors, **Dimitris Trivolis-Pieris** (1785-1809) and **Ioannis-Vaptistis Kalosgouros** (1794-1878), who was also an architect and painter. Much later, the Corfiot artist **Evangelos Kallos** (1861-1931), a faithful exponent of the Classical approach, distinguished himself in sculpture.

In painting, the tradition of the Ionian school - whose last true representative was N. Kantounis (see p. 110) - continued for a long period to produce works which reflected the spirit of nineteenth century Italian art. Among the painters of this period, a distinctive position is occupied by **Gerasimos Pitzimanos** (1787-1825), from Cephalonia, who was also a sculptor (and a pupil of Canova), an architect and an engineer. He taught architecture in Prosalentis' school and painted more than 200 water-colours, some of which were in the tradition established by Kantounis while others reveal a strong influence from French Romanticism. The pupils of Prosalentis included **Dionysios Veyias** (1819-1884), of Cephalonia, who inclined principally towards portrait-painting and historical compositions, and **Spyridon Prosalentis**, Pavlos' son (1830-1895), who painted numerous portraits of leading figures in the War of Independence and functioned within a framework of academicism. Spyridon's son **Aimilios Prosalentis** (1859-1926) is another interesting painter, whose main subjects were historical naval scenes. Also of importance was **Charalambos Pachis**

(1844-1891), who founded his own school of art in Corfu. He distinguished himself in the fields of landscape and genre painting, both of which he introduced into the Ionian school. Pachis passed the tradition of landscape painting on to his pupils **Periklis Tsirigiotis** (1865-1924), who travelled in Egypt and painted many landscapes from that country, **Georgios Samartzis** (1868-1925), the water-colourist **Angelos Yallinos** (1857-1939), whose paintings were a hymn of praise to the Corfiot landscape and who founded a school of painting, and **Spyros Skarvelis** (1868-1942), who was among the artists involved in the decoration of the Achilleio and distinguished himself as a water-colourist.

Corfu produced a number of important painters and engravers in subsequent generations. The most notable names here are the copper engravers **Markos Zavitsianos** (1844-1923), **Lykourgos Kogevinas** (1887-1940), and **Dimitris Galanis** (1879-1966). The major artists of Corfu during this period included a woman painter, **Maria Desylla-Lavranou** (1893-1987), who worked chiefly in the field of portaiture. The last great Corfiot artist of the twentieth century was **Nikolaos Ventouras** (1899-1990), an engraver and lithographer who with unique skill succeeded in giving his works - most of them landscapes - an abstractive air.

5. THE TOWN TODAY

Corfu town, the capital of the island, has a population of around 30,000 and is the centre of economic, political and cultural life for the Corfiots. It is the chief town of the Prefecture of Corfu, and as such is the location of most of the public authorities (banks, law-courts, prisons, hospital, consulates, the National Tourist Organisation, etc.). It is the seat of the Metropolitan Bishop of Corfu and Paxoi, whose official church is St Spyridon. A complete educational system consists of primary and secondary schools (junior and senior), private schools, foreign-language schools, vocational training schools, and a university (the Ionian University, with departments of Foreign Languages, Translation and Interpreting, Music, and History). There is a good public transport network, with town buses and services to nearly all the villages. There are daily flights and ferry departures to other parts of Greece and other countries, which facilitate the highly-developed commerce and tourism of the island.

The large numbers of tourists who visit Corfu each year give the island a cosmopolitan air. In order to meet the needs of the tourist trade, many hotel and apartment units have been constructed in recent decades; these are fully-equipped and comply fully with modern requirements. Shops and other establishments dedicated to the tourist industry are to be found all over the town, together with quaint tavernas and de luxe restaurants, old-style coffee-shops and modern outdoor cafes, and discos and bars which are open until late into the night. There is a casino in the Corfu Hilton International hotel, while there are also football pitches, golf courses and tennis courts, a stadium, a swimming-pool and a Yacht Club, all open to visitors as well as local people. The beaches at Mon Repos and the Yacht Club are suitable for swimming and sea sports.

p. 131
A street in the commercial district of Corfu town.

The Corfiots have been known since ancient times for their love of song, dance and merrymaking. Today they hold frequent cultural events and festivals each year. Their religious feasts are of particular interest, consisting of services and processions through the town to the accompaniment of music played by the town band. The procession of St Spyridon (see p. 100) and that in which the icon of Our Lady is carried round the town on 15 August rival Easter itself in the number of people whom they attract to the alleys and churches of Corfu and in the atmosphere of devotion which they create. The religious parts of these feasts are accompanied by secular merrymaking, with much eating, singing and dancing. The anniversary of the union of the Dodecanese with Greece is celebrated on 21 May each year, while the festivities of the Carnival occupy the last three Sundays before the beginning of Lent. During the summer, there are lectures, concerts, theatrical productions and performances of folk dancing and ballets. From May to September, a 'Son et Lumière' event is held at the Old Fortress, and on 10 August the so-called 'Barcarola' is celebrated. In September, the Corfu Festival attracts the participation of artists and ensembles from all over Greece and from other countries, and games of cricket against visiting English

pp. 132-133

The Corfiots are famous for their busy social life and the many events they organise, always focusing on the Spianada. In the photographs, religious processions, parades and cricket matches in Corfu.

teams are often held on the Spianada during the summer months.

The centre of all these events, and indeed of social life in Corfu more generally, has for centuries been the **Spianada**. Divided by Dousmani St into the Upper and Lower Piazza, the Spianada is surrounded by some of the most notable monuments in Corfu and has a superb view of the Municipal Gardens, the Contrafossa and the Old Fortress, on its eastern side. On the west side, cafes and restaurants operate beneath the arches of the Liston, and visitors can enjoy their coffee or try one of the specialities of the local cuisine ('pastitsada' beef with

p. 134
A train for children in the alleyways of the old town.

spaghetti, 'sofrito' beef with garlic, fish in a 'bourdeto' sauce), washed down with a good island wine or perhaps with ginger-beer, one of the relics of the period of British rule. On the Spianada, traditional horse-drawn carriages are available for hire, and the driver provides a tour of some of the prettier parts of town.

North of the Spianada - behind the Palace - begins Arseniou St, which runs above the sea-front through the district called the **Mourayia**, along the Venetian sea-walls. There is a wonderful view from here across to the coast of Albania. The sea-front road, now called Athinagora St,

leads down to the **harbour**, one of the busiest in Greece. Not far out at sea is the islet called **Vido**, ancient Ptychia, to which caiques ply daily. Until 1864, there was a Venetian fortress on Vido. Now it is disused. Above the harbour towers the hill on which stands the New Fortress, with its Venetian outworks. At 7-9 Solomou St, close to the entrance to the New Fortress, is a modern museum of considerable interest: the **Maritime Museum** of Napoleondas Sayias. Founded in 1989 with exhibits which its owner had collected from all over the world, it contains shells, pieces of coral, fossils, shark jaws, crabs, lobsters, snakes, starfish, sponges, micro-organisms and much more.

The most unforgettable experience awaiting the visitor is, however, a stroll through the centre of Corfu town and in particular through the old-world **Campiello district**. The narrow alleys ('kantounia') lined with tall buildings, often spanned by arches or by the washing-lines of the townsfolk, the attractive little squares with their carved stone wells, the churches with their elegant bell-towers, and the occasional mansion with skilfully-wrought balconies and hanging lanterns help to create a medieval atmosphere to be found nowhere else in Greece. Of al-

p. 135
A carriage-ride to Mourayia is an unforgettable experience for Greeks and visitors alike.

most equal interest is the **market**, in the streets to the west of the Spianada: Nikiforou Theotoki St, spanned with arches ('volta'), still retains many traces of the Venetian period. The Ionian Bank building, at the intersection of N. Theotoki and Filarmonikis Sts, houses a **collection of banknotes** covering the period from Turkish times down to the present day. There is also an exhibition of photographs showing how coins are minted.

Despite the number of new buildings that have been constructed to meet the needs of tourism and the merciless destruction that others have undergone over the centuries - culminating in the German bombing raids of 1943 - Corfu can still boast private and public buildings of the greatest value for the Greek cultural heritage. In every corner of the town are traces of all those whose fate it was to tread the ground of the island and add another piece to the mosaic of its history. Since 1976, Corfu town has been on the list of Europe's most historic cities, and efforts are still being made to conserve as much as possible of its historic atmosphere. An enormous programme of maintenance work on the monuments of Corfu began in 1992-1994, on the occasion of the town being chosen as the venue for the European Union summit meeting during the Greek Presidency of the Community.

pp. 136-137
Scenes from the everyday life of the people of Corfu.

THE ACHILLEIO

GASTOURI - ACHILLEIO

Gastouri is a small village close to the sea, 11.5 km. south of Corfu town. In the village square, beneath a tree, is the so-called Spring of Elizabeth, which has now run dry.

The whole area is connected with the **Empress Elizabeth of Austria,** often known as Sissy, whose summer palace, the famous Achilleio, stands a mere two kilometres from Gastouri. The life of the Empress Elizabeth (1837-1898) has repeatedly been the subject of novels and films, as a result of her beauty, her strength of character, and the story of her love for the Emperor Franz Josef. Elizabeth married the Austrian Emperor in 1854, and the couple had two daughters, Sophia and Gisela, and a son called Rudolf. But Elizabeth's liberal notions displeased her mother-in-law, the Archduchess Sophia, who personally took in hand the upbringing of the royal children and denied their mother access to them. Such little contact as there had been between the children and their mother came to an

pp. 138-139

The Achilleio, the luxurious palace built by the Empress Elizabeth of Austria, as it is today.

p. 140

Above: one of the verandas on the facade of the Achilleio.

Below: the staircase with the statues of the gods; from right to left, Aphrodite, Apollo, Hermes and Artemis.

abrupt end when, on one of the journeys of the Imperial couple, young Sophia died and Elizabeth was held responsible for the tragedy. Her health broken, she travelled to Madeira to recuperate, and on her way back to Austria (in 1861) stopped off at Corfu, whose beauty made an immediate impression on her. In the summer of the same year, Elizabeth returned to the island and stayed at Mon Repos, returning in the autumn to Vienna to give birth to Valeria, her last daughter. Over this period, she began to take a much greater interest in politics. In 1869, Franz Josef and Elizabeth were declared monarchs of Hungary. In 1876, Elizabeth travelled

on her own to Athens and Corfu and threw herself into a study of ancient Greek literature - especially of Homer. She also took a keen interest in the excavations being carried out at the time by Heinrich Schliemann in Troy, Mycenae and Tiryns. After a long trip to Troy and many other parts of the ancient Greek world, she returned to Corfu in 1888 and stayed as a guest in the Vrailas villa. A year later, Elizabeth bought the estate and began work on the construction of the palace - in an atmosphere of profound mourning, because in the meantime her son Rudolf and his lover had been found dead. During her time at the Achilleio, Elizabeth learned

pp. 140-141
The verdant gardens of the Achilleio, with the statue of 'Achilles Triumphant'.

p. 142

The staircase in the reception room of the Achilleio, flanked by bronze statues of Zeus and Hera. In the background, stucco sculptures of the gods of Olympus.

p. 143

The fresco by Galopi on the subject of 'The Four Seasons and the Hours' on the ceiling of the reception room.

the Greek language and much about the ancient literature from eminent teachers, notable among whom was the scholar and writer Constantinos Christomanos, who was officially employed for this purpose by the Imperial court. In 1898, the 'melancholy queen', as Elizabeth had come to be called, was assassinated in a hotel in Geneva by an Italian anarchist.

Elizabeth called her palace at Gastouri **the Achilleio**, dedicating it to her favourite hero, Achilles; as she herself wrote, *"he represents the Greek spirit, the beauty of the land"*, and is *"as strong, as proud and as obstinate as a Greek mountain"*. The Achilleio was constructed in 1889-1891, by the Italian architects Rafael Corito and Antonio Lanti, under the personal supervision of the Empress, who also took charge of the ornamentation of the palace with paintings and sculptures, most of which were purchased from the Borghese family. It is a luxurious three-storey building in the 'Pompeian

p. 144

Above: the room with the collection of mementoes of the Empress Elizabeth.

Below: the sanctuary apse in the Empress's Catholic chapel.

order', with neo-Classical elements, and it is surrounded by densely-vegetated gardens adorned with important works of art. In 1908, after the death of Elizabeth, the Achilleio was bought by Wilhelm II, the German Kaiser, and in 1914 - on the outbreak of the First World War - it was abandoned. In 1915, it was used as the headquarters of the Serbian Army and as a hospital, coming into the hands of the Greek state in 1919. During the Second World War it served as a hospital again - and as the headquarters of the German and Italian occupying forces - and after liberation it houses a variety of schools and institutions. Today, it belongs to the National Tourist Organisation and from 1962 to 1992 Corfu casino operated there. The ground floor of the building functions as a museum.

We enter the Achilleio through an iron *gate* ornamented with two bronze reliefs, of Zeus (left) and Achilles (right). The first room on the ground floor, the *reception hall*, has a fresco in the centre of its ceiling, by the Italian painter Galopi, on the theme of *The Four Seasons* and the *Hours*. Also of interest in this room are the Italian marble fireplace, two statuettes of Athena and Hebe (above the fireplace, by the German sculptore Heinemann), and a painting of Elizabeth by the German artist Witterhalter. At the far end of the reception hall, a magnificent staircase flanked by bronze statues of Zeus and Hera and by a large collection of marble and plaster sculptures (of Zeus, Niobe, Artemis, Apollo, Aphrodite, Hermes and Pan) leads to the upper floors. To the right of the reception room is the Empress's *Catholic chapel.* In the sanctuary apse are representations of Christ and Pontius Pilate, beneath which is an icon of Christ and Our Lady (by Franz Matz). There are two recesses with statues of Christ and Our Lady, an altar and a harmonium. Next to the chapel is a *room with mementoes of Elizabeth*: medallions, photographs, paintings, candlesticks, furniture, a

p. 145

The last room on the ground floor, containing Elizabeth's furniture. Above: her desk. Below: her chaise-longe, her mirrors, and a painting by L. Thiers of 'Odysseus and Nausicaa'.

portrait of the Empress, two poems written by her, and a bust of Franz Josef. The next room contains some of the *personal effects of Wilhelm II*: his desk, a stove, a wash-hand basin, a mirror, plates, medals, documents, three paintings of ships and the Kaiser, photographs, etc. A small room in the left wing of the Museum leads to the *palace banqueting hall*, a few parts of whose original decoration have remained. Here there are more mementoes of Elizabeth and Franz Josef: photographs, a sword, a clock, a mirror, etc. The rococo furnishings are from the time of Kaiser Wilhelm. Of interest in the next *small room* are five sculptures on mythological themes (the Apple of Discord, Paris and Helen, Sappho, Or-

p. 146
Above: the room with mementoes of Kaiser Wilhelm II.
Below: Elizabeth's dining-room.

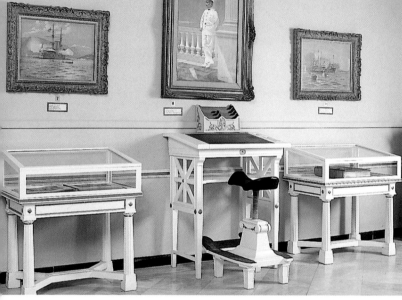

pheus and Eurydice, and Dionysus with his entourage) and two
sculptured amphorae. The *last
room* on the ground floor contains Elizabeth's desk, bookcase,
chaise-longue and other items of
furniture, three carved mirrors,
bronze statues and busts, photographs, pieces of jewellery and an
oil-painting on the theme of the
meeting on Scheria between
Odysseus and Nausicaa (Ludwig
Thiers).

The grand staircase ends, on the
top floor, in a *balcony* with an
Ionic peristyle ornamented with
busts and with statues of the Nine
Muses. The wall above the balcony is decorated with an impressive painting of *The Triumph of
Achilles*, by the German painter
Franz Matz. Achilles is shown up-

pp. 146-147
*The fine wall-
painting of 'The
Triumph of
Achilles', by
Franz Matz.*

p. 148
The Ionic peristyle on the rear veranda of the Achilleio, with the statues of the Nine Muses.

right on his chariot as he races in triumph around the walls of Troy, dragging the body of Hector behind him and holding the dead man's helmet. (As Homer tells us in the *Iliad*, from which the painter was inspired for this scene, Achilles killed Hector and dishonoured his corpse in this way in vengeance for Hector's having killed Achilles' beloved friend Patroclus in battle.) The horses of Achilles are strikingly rendered, and the entire composition is very vigorous.

The *gardens* of the Achilleio are among the most beautiful places on Corfu and enjoy a superb view across to the Kanoni, Pontikonisi, the Chalkiopoulou lagoon and Mt Pantokrator. They, too, are a kind of open-air muse-

um, being full of outstanding sculptures. Notable among this statuary are compositions showing Apollo, Hermes, Artemis and Aphrodite near the entrance to the palace, the statues of the Nine Muses and the Graces in the Ionic peristyle of the rear veranda, the busts of ancient philosophers and poets behind the columns of the peristyle, the marble statue of Lord Byron on the topmost balcony on the side facing the forest, and the statue of Elizabeth herself close to the sea. However, the most important statues in the grounds of the Achilleio are the *Dying Achilles* and the *Triumphant Achilles*. The former of these originally stood on the large terrace in the gardens, where the latter is now located.

pp. 148-149

The outstanding statue of the 'Dying Achilles', by Ernst Herter, 'trademark' of the Achilleio.

p. 150
The natural platform in front of the peristyle of the Muses on which the 'Dying Achilles' stands.

p. 151
The colossal statue of the 'Triumphant Achilles' by the German sculptor Getz. Unlike the 'Dying Achilles', which reflects Elizabeth's sensitivity, this work represents the concentrated power of Wilhelm II.

Kaiser Wilhelm decided to move the *Dying Achilles* because it was too small to ensure that it could be seen among the tall palm trees. After moving it, he installed the *Triumphant Achilles* on its former position; this is an enormous bronze statue, eleven metres in height, on a tall marble plinth, which was created in 1909 by the German sculptor Getz and was so heavy that it had to be moved to Corfu in sections and assembled on the spot. Achilles is shown in triumph - a pose suitable for a ruler as powerful as Wilhelm - and upright, with his shield, his spear and his helmet.

The *Dying Achilles* now stands on the terrace in front of, and slightly below, the peristyle with the Muses. It is a marble statue by the German sculptor Ernst Herder, made to a commission by Elizabeth in 1884, and originally located in her palace in Vienna. Achilles here is semi-recumbent, almost nude, wearing his helmet and attempting to draw the fatal arrow shot by Paris from his heel. This outstanding work, now the established emblem of the Achilleio, is notable for the skill with which the artist has rendered the hero's anguish and pain as death approaches.

ΑΧΙΛΛΕΥΣ

LANDSCAPES ON THE ISLAND

C orfu town is not the only place to have monuments; they are to be found all over the island as incontrovertible witnesses to the brilliance of its history. Nor does the modern era lag behind in any way, for the countryside of Corfu is a succession of landscapes of unrivalled beauty. The island is densely wooded, with olive groves that convey an air of serenity and go some way towards masking the steeply plunging cliffs of the west and with idyllic mountain hamlets peeping out of the greenery higher up the hills. Along the coast, the tone is set by quaint fishing-villages built close to the water's edge, or near sandy beaches where bathers in their hundreds enjoy the sun and the cool sea. In the summer months, the constantly increasing tourist industry makes Corfu buzz, but there is no shortage of more isolated corners which hold out against modern developments and retain much of their authenticity. There, the serenity of the landscape bring earth and sky closer together and the aromas borne on the wind remind us that this is a place the gods have touched.

1. KANONI - PERAMA

p. 153

The area around Kanoni, with Vlacherna Monastery and Pontikonisi in the background.

Towards the south end of Corfu town is gently-curving **Garitsa bay**, whose shore is an ideal place for a stroll or a trip in a horse-drawn carriage. At the south end of Garitsa bay stands the Kanoni promontory, where most of the oldest monuments of Corfu are concentrated. Those closest to the town are the circular **cenotaph of Menecrates** (see p. 54) and the **church of Sts**

Jason and Sosipater (see p. 75). Not far away is the **Palaiopoli district**, where the ancient city of Corcyra stood (see p. 50). Further to the west, near the ancient **Hyllaean harbour**, are the remains of the **temple of Artemis** (see p. 53), while in Palaiopoli itself, by the entrance to Mon Repos, we can see what has remained of the Early Christian **basilica of St Cercyra** (see p. 74). The densely-wooded **Mon Repos estate** was used after 1831 as the summer residence of High Commissioner Frederick Adam, and later belonged to the Greek royal family (see p. 50). Inside it, the High Commissioner's miniature palace has survived, and archaeologists have excavated the Kardaki temple and the temple of Hera. At Kardaki, close to the sea, is the spring by the same name which supplied the ancient city with water. Today, there is a fountain there, with a lion's-head spout, from which rushes a constant flow of cool water. Lorenzos Mavilis describes the **Kardaki spring** in one of his finest sonnets, while there is also a folk saying according to which, *"any stranger who wets his lips at the spring will never return home to his own people"*. Above Kardaki rises **Analipsi hill**, with a magical view across the sea to the coast of Epirus and also north over Corfu itself. The village of Analipsi is the site of the ancient acropolis, on which a few traces of buildings still remain.

At the southern end of the promontory, 4 km. from the centre of Corfu town, is **Kanoni**, a place of international renown. It took its name from a cannon which the French set up there. Although Kanoni is one of the busiest places on the island and despite the number of hotels and other tourist facilities that cluster around it, it is still as picturesque as ever thanks to its unique view. Below the viewpoint, a metal bridge leads out from the promontory to an islet on which stands the seventeenth-century **Vlacherna Monastery**, Corfu's immediately-recognisable trademark. Further out is another islet, **Pontikonisi**, whose clump of cypress trees has served as a source of inspiration for artists from all over the world. According to tradition, the islet was originally the ship of the Phaeacians which Poseidon turned to stone as it sailed back from taking Odysseus to Ithaca. On Pontikonisi stands the Byzantine **church of Christ Pantocrator** (eleventh-twelfth century), to which there is a pilgrimage on 6 August. Caiques from Kanoni take visitors out to Pontikonisi through the summer months.

From Kanoni, a narrow bridge runs across the Chalkiopoulou lagoon (the ancient Hyllaean harbour), close to the end of the runway of Corfu airport, and ends on the other side of the lagoon at **Perama**. This is a small tourist village set among olive trees, with good swimming beaches.

pp. 155-156
Views from Kanoni: the picturesque Vlacherna Monastery and the densely-wooded islet of Pontikonisi.

2. BENITSES-
MORAITIKA-
MESONGI - CHLOMOS-
KORISSION LAGOON

p. 158
The tourist resort of
Benitses.

p. 159
Above: view of
Benitses.
Below: the village of
Mesongi and
its beach.

Close to Gastouri, 13 km. south of Corfu town, is **Benitses**, once a small village but in recent years a centre for tourist development and a place whose night-life is renowned. The village stands in an area rich in orange and lemon trees and has a pebble beach. The remains of a Roman baths have been excavated in the area, and a Roman villa (of the third century AD) with a mosaic floor has come to light. **Moraitika,** another former fishing village, is now equally cosmopolitan in atmosphere. It is 7 km. south of Benitses and has a sandy beach. Here, too, a Roman house has been discovered; it may well have been the summer residence of an Imperial official. At **Mesongi**, 2 km. further along the road south, there is a long beach and a camp site, and the little Mesongi River flows into the sea close to the village. A turning near Mesongi leads to **Chlomos**, consisting of old houses built on a hill. A turning in the other direction will take us to the **Korission lagoon**, separated from the sea by sandhills which have an

excellent beach on their outer side. The lagoon is now a scheduled wetland and serves as a natural breeding-ground for fish. A few specimens of the threatened *Caretta caretta* species of turtle have also made their home here.

3. ARGYRADES - LEFKIMMI - KAVOS

Argyrades, 33 km. south of Corfu town, is one of the largest villages on the island and is interesting for its traditional architecture, in which many features dating back to the Venetian period can be distinguished. To the south-west is the long and attractive beach of **Ayios Yeorgios**, but the whole area is well-known for its beaches with their fine sand (including Marathia, Maltas near the village of Perivoli, and Gardenios near Vitalades). To the north-west of Argyrades, at a distance of 3 km., is the pretty fishing-village of **Petriti**, where there is almost always fresh fish to be had. However, the largest community in south Corfu is **Lefkimmi,** 42 km. from Corfu town, which has a population of 5,000. It stands in a fertile area dense with olives and vineyards, where some of the island's best wine is made. On the out-

skirts of the town is the convent of **Our Lady of the Angels**, founded in 1696 by the Varlaam family in thanksgiving for having been saved during a storm at sea. The convent holds its feast day on 15 August, while Lefkimmi itself celebrates St Procopius' day on 8 July and also holds riotous festivities at Carnival time. There are ferry boats from Lefkimmi har-

pp. 160-161

The south coast of Corfu. Right: anchorage at Lefkimmi. Above: the village of Petriti. Below: the beach at Kavos.

bour to Igoumenitsa, on the mainland coast. A further 4 km. from Lefkimmi brings us to **Kavos**, a small village which stands amongst huge olive trees and cypresses. In recent years, thanks to its wide sandy beach, Kavos has developed into a major tourist centre. Small boats operate up the coast from Kavos to Corfu town, and in the other direction to the island of Paxi. Nearby (2 km. from Kavos), is cape Asprokavos, the southernmost point on the island, with the **monastery of Our Lady 'Arkoudila'** standing in a prominent position on top of Arkoudila hill, where there is a superb view. The monastery is a fortified structure, built in 1700 by the Varlaam family in further commemoration of their salvation.

4. GARDIKI - AYIOS MATTHAIOS

A road leads off from the bridge at Mesongi to Ayios Matthaios, and from it another turning brings us to the spot known as Gardiki. The principal attraction of **Gardiki** is a ruined Byzantine castle of the thirteenth century, octagonal in shape and with eight imposing towers. Two of the towers have interesting ornamental brickwork built into their walls, and here and there throughout the entire structure are architectural members from ancient buildings that once stood round about. Another turning before we reach Ayios Matthaios crosses the slopes of the hill called Mathios. The hill is also known as the Gamelion Horos ('Wedding Mountain') because of the tradition that the marriage of Alcinous and Arete took place there. On the hill stands the **monastery of Christ Pantocrator**, some 500 metres from which is the **Cave of Pelaou**, which is believed to run as far as the sea. Inside the cave, traces of human habitation in the Palaeolithic era have been discovered. **Ayios Matthaios** (22.5 km. from Corfu town) is a large village on a naturally amphitheatrical site, surrounded by a wood of oak trees and olives.

p. 162
The rocky coast rises steeply behind the beach at Ayios Gordios. In the background, the rock called Ortholithi.

5. PAVLIANA - GAROUNA - AYIOS GORDIOS - SINARADES

Ano ('upper') Pavliana is an inland village which stands on a verdant hill. Kato ('lower') Pavliana is very close at hand. In the church of St Demetrius - which has a well-attended feast day on 26 October - is an interesting iconostasis carved out of stone by the Kardamis family of sculptors. Another sculpture by the same family is to be found in the village of **Garouna (Ano and Kato)**, which has a particular tradition in this art. The statue, created by Stefanos Kardamis in memory of his late father, depicts that self-taught stonemason. Garouna, also known for its carpet-weaving workshop, is the venue - in mid-August - of lectures, performances, competitions and mountain-climbing contest. **Ayios Gordios**, on the coast below Garouna, is one of the most popular resort areas on the island; it has a sandy beach some five kilometres long, with strange rock formations at either end and green hills on the landward side. Of particular interest is Ortholithi, an isolated rock in the sea, about which there is a short story by Iakovos Polylas. Three kilometres from Ayios Gordios is the village of **Sinarades**, which has the only **Folk-lore Museum** on the island. Located in a traditional village house, it contains a reconstruction of a typical nineteenth-century rural dwelling.

p. 163
Exhibits in the Folklore Museum at Sinarades.

6. PELEKAS - GLYFADA - ERMONES

Pelekas, an old-style village 13.5 km. to the south-west of Corfu town, stands on the top of an idyllic hill with an amazing view. At the highest point of the village is a flat area called 'the Kaiser's throne', since Wilhelm II often made his way to Pelekas to admire the unforgettable sunset. The view at sundown - out to sea, over the interior of the island and even as far as Corfu town - is a unique experience. Pelekas is something of a resort area, thanks partly to the fine beach not far away at **Glyfada** (3 km.). It takes about 45 minutes to walk from Glyfada to the **monastery of Our Lady 'Myrtiotissa'**, which stands among olive groves, cypresses and banana trees (the only ones on the island; the fruit they produce is

p. 164
Below: the beach at Glyfada.
Right: sunset at Pelekas.

small, but extremely tasty). The monastery is said to have been founded in the fourteenth century by a Turk who converted to Christianity and to have taken its name from an icon of Our Lady found in a clump of myrtles. The monastery holds its feast-day on 24 September each year. The beach at Myrtiotissa is one of the finest on Corfu; very few people

go there, the water is cool and clean, the beach is sandy and the whole area is set about with pine trees. To the north of Myrtiotissa is yet another beautiful bay, whose beach is called **Ermones**. The landscape here is imposing, with steep cliffs and wooded hills, and it is said to have inspired the poet Lorentzos Mavilis. According to one version of the story, Ermones was the place where Odysseus was washed ashore, and where he met Nausicaa and her companions. Traces of human habitation in the Neolithic and Mycenean periods have come to light in the vicinity. At the village of **Vatos**, near Ermones, is a camp site, and further north, in the **Ropa valley**, is Corfu golf course.

p. 165
The beaches of Ermones (above) and Glyfada (below).

7. PALAIOKASTRITSA - LAKONES - ANGELOKASTRO

Palaiokastritsa is one of the most picturesque - and busiest - places on Corfu, and has been a famous resort area since the period of British rule. The village is spread around six little bays (Ambelaki, Ayios Petros, Ayios Spyridon, Alipa, Platakia, Ayia Triada) all of which have sandy beaches and caves and are backed by verdant hills covered with olive trees. The beaches of Palaiokastritsa are very popular with bathers, who when not engaging in the sea sports available there can try fresh lobster - for which the area is famous - at one of the numerous little tavernas. Caiques sail from these bays to a number of other nearby coves which are not accessible by land. In the sea are the islets of Skeloudi and Kolovri; a story connected with Kolovri tells us that it was the ship of some Algerian pirates which was turned to stone by divine intervention to prevent the pirates from attacking the monastery of Palaiokastritsa. Some archaeologists believe that the city of the Phaeacians and the palace of Alcinous were actually somewhere near Palaiokastritsa. Their views are not, however, generally accepted. According to these scholars, the acropolis of Scheria would have been on the hill now occupied by

pp. 166-167
A view of the verdant landscape at Palaiokastritsa.

the **monastery of Our Lady the Mother of God.** The monastery was founded in 1228, but the buildings we see today date from no earlier than the eighteenth and nineteenth centuries. The arched courtyard is very beautiful, as is the view out over the bays of Palaiokastritsa. The monastery church was built in 1722 and is a single-aisled basilica. It has an in-

p. 168
The Monastery of
Our Lady at
Palaiokastritsa.

teresting collection of icons dating from the fifteenth to the eighteenth century. More notable Byzantine and post-Byzantine icons, together with vestments, sacred books and holy vessels, are housed in the little monastery museum.

Not far from Palaiokastritsa (4 km.) is the village of **Lakones**, where the spot called **Bella Vista** has a panoramic view of the deeply

indented coast around Palaiokas-tritsa. The road continues to the village of **Krini**, from which a path leads in 3 km. to the superb fortress of **Angelokastro**. Angelokastro, one of the few Byzantine castles of Corfu, was built in the thirteenth century by Michael I Angelus Ducas, ruler of the Despotate of Epirus, to protect Corfu against the incursions of pirates.

Not much has survived of the buildings inside the castle, but the climb up to the top of the precipitous hill on which it stands is worth the effort for the incredible view out to sea and east towards Corfu town. The road between Palaiokastritsa and Corfu town - a smooth run of some 25 km. - was built by the British in 1828 to improve their control over the area.

p. 169

The deeply-indented coastline, beaches and densely-wooded hillsides of Palaiokastritsa.

Below right: Angelokastro.

8. ALYKES - GOUVIA - DASIA - IPSOS

p. 170

The promontory on which the village of Gouvia stands.

p. 171

Above: the highly-developed beach at Kontokali.

Below: luxury hotel accommodation along the beach at Dasia.

The bay which lies to the north of Corfu town actually consists of a large number of little coves, around whose gently-sloping shores stand attractive and busy tourist resorts. Among the most highly developed of these is **Alykes** (4 km.), a coastal village with luxury hotel complexes. From Alykes, a road runs to the village of **Potamos** and '**The Village**', a modern reconstruction of a traditional Corfiot village of Venetian times. In late summer, the wine festival is held at 'The Village', and the year's wines may be tasted - free of charge - to the accompaniment of performances of music. Not far away is the village of **Evropouli**, site of the **Capodistrias Museum** with its collection of the personal effects of the man who was the first governor of modern Greece. More tourist amenities are to be found at **Kontokali** (8 km.), which stands on a small bay and has a marina for pleasure craft, some good beaches and a camp site. One kilometre further north is the long sandy beach belonging to the village of **Gouvia**. On the way to this area from Corfu town, we pass the Venetian naval base, of which some ruins have

survived together with those of a fortress. Off Kontokali and Gouvia is the islet of **Lazareto**, which from the fourteenth to the eighteenth century was the quarantine station for the crews of ships arriving in Corfu. The next beaches in this direction are those of **Dafnila** and **Dasia,** both of which are backed by olive groves that run almost down to the sea. The Club Med facilities are at Dasia, and not far away, at the **Villa Mimbelli**, is a replica of a fourteenth-century Italian *palazzo*. Of equal tourist interest is the village of **Ipsos**, which stands behind a long beach at the very foot of Mt Pantokrator.

9. SKRIPERO - KORAKIANA - AYIOS MARKOS - PYRGI

pp. 172-173
Views of the sandy, green-fringed beaches of Corfu: above, Ipsos and Dasia. Below, right: a Venetian building at Dafnilas. Below, left: the Kommeno promontory.

Skripero is an attractive, traditional village in the interior of the island (approximately 8 km. from Gouvia), with a fine view. There is a feast and a banquet for all the village on 4 December, when the church of St Barbara celebrates its saint's day. Two km. from Skripero is Ano Korakiana, another quaint village which is noted for its numerous churches. They include the churches of St George, with a carved marble iconostasis and icons by C. Pachis and Y. Samartzis (nineteenth cen-

tury), of St Athanasius with Byzantine wall-paintings (fifteenth century), of St James (fifteenth century), and of the Archangel Michael. Many of the icons from these churches are now on show in the Antivouniotissa Museum in Corfu town. The sights in **Ano Korakiana** (which has a tradition in choral music) also include: an interesting potter's workshop in the Feleka district, the mansion of the author Iakovos Polylas (at the foot of the hill called Korakio), and the primary school, a neo-Classical building dating from 1932 and housing a small folklore collection. In the first ten days of August each year, the local people hold an exhibition of paintings. Close to Ano Korakiana (3 km.) is **Kato Korakiana**, a little seaside village which has been developed for tourism. Another road from Ano Korakiana leads to the village of A**yios Markos**, where there

p. 175

The vernacular architectural tradition has survived in many of the mountain villages of Corfu. In the illustrations: village houses whose courtyards are full of flowers.

are two important Christian monuments: the church of Christ Pantocrator, with wall-paintings of 1576, and the church of St Mercurius, whose wall-paintings date back to 1075. This road continues and in 2 km. comes out on the coast at **Pyrgi**, which shares with Ipsos the long beach called 'The Golden Mile' by the local people.

10. SPARTILAS - STRINILAS-PANTOCRATOR MONASTERY

Outside Pyrgi is the turning which heads into the interior of the island and up to the mountain villages of **Spartilas** and **Strinilas**. This is a route of breath-taking splendour, and the views down the mountainside and out to sea are most impressive. Even finer prospects are to be had from the peak of Mt Pantokrator (906 m.): when the weather permits, the coast of Epirus and Albania can be seen to the east, the little islands of Ereikoussa, Othoni and Mathraki are visible to the west, and even Paxi and Lefkada, far to the south, can be discerned. The summit is crowned with the **Pantocrator monastery**, first founded in 1347 and destroyed in the sixteenth century. Although it was rebuilt in 1689, almost nothing of the building's earlier stages has survived. Inside is a collection of post-Byzantine icons.

11. BARBATI - NISAKI-KALAMI - KOULOURA-AYIOS STEFANOS

p. 176
The beaches at Barbati (left) and Nisaki (right).

p. 177
The bays of Kalami (above) and Kouloura (below).

Along the north-east coast of Corfu are numerous little bays by which stand seaside villages and attractive tavernas where one can enjoy fresh fish and the view across the narrow channel to the coast of Albania. **Barbati** is a wide bay with a fine sandy beach, while **Nisaki**'s beach is pebbly and there are caique sailings to Corfu town. Not far to the north is the picturesque bay of **Kalami**, where the author Lawrence Durrell lived while writing *Prospero's Cave*. His house can still be seen. Next comes the bay of **Kouloura**, a most attractive little harbour where there is a fortified Venetian house. A side-road beyond Kouloura leads to the little cove of **Ayios Stefanos**, whose cape is the nearest point on Corfu to the Albanian mainland; the channel is only 1.5 miles wide at this point.

12. KASSIOPI

Kassiopi is a large and attractive village by the sea beneath the lower slopes of Mt Pantokrator, 37 km. to the north of Corfu town. It is now a busy tourist resort. In Roman times, the site was occupied by a flourishing city which we know from the written sources to have had a harbour, a theatre and a temple to Zeus Cassios, which is probably the origin of the name Kassiopi. This city was visited by many eminent figures of the Roman era, including Cicero and Ptolemy, and there is a tradition that the Emperor Nero prayed and sang before the altar of Zeus Cassios. A Christian church of **Our Lady 'Kassiotissa'** was later built on the site once occupied by the temple of Zeus. This building was de-stroyed by fire in 1537 and reconstructed in 1590. Inside it is an important icon of *Our Lady with Christ*, the work of T. Poulakis (seventeenth century). On 15 August the church is the scene of a major feast, with services and celebrations lasting all night. On a hill above the town are the ruins of a castle built by the Angevins in the thirteenth century, which was one of the strongest on the island in its day. There are sailings by launch from Kassiopi to the islands of Othoni, Ereikoussa and Mathraki.

13. ALMYROS - ACHARAVI - RODA

The north part of Corfu looks quite different from the rest of the island, partly because there is less tourism. The landscape is still most attractive, combining the allure of mountains and the sea alike, and the inhabitants are strongly attached to their traditions. The coastal area of **Almyros** is of great archaeological interest because of the cemetery which has been discovered there and is still being excavated. The burials date from between the late Archaic and Hellenistic periods and the cemetery belonged to a farming community whose economy seems to have had little contact with the outside world.

p. 178

Kassiopi beach.

p. 179

Views of the villages of Ayios Stefanos (above) and Kassiopi (below).

To the west of Almyros is a vast sandy beach (Ayios Yeorgios bay) and there is a lagoon (lake Antinioti) of ecological interest. By the coast are the pleasant little villages of **Acharavi** and **Roda;** in the latter, archaeologists have excavated a temple of the fifth century BC whose architectural members are on display in Corfu Archaeological Museum.

14. KAROUSADES - SIDARI - AYIOS YEORGIOS

From Roda, there is a road leading into the interior of the island and to the quaint village of **Karousades**. In the village is the mansion of the Theotokis family, a dynasty which produced many of Corfu's leading figures in the artistic as well as the political world. The building is fortified, and must first have been built in the fifteenth century. The coast road continues in 5 km. to **Sidari**, a former fishing village whose beaches are of unrivalled beauty. There are rock formations of a particularly striking nature which form a huge number of tiny coves and narrow channels. One of them, of distinctive beauty, is called the 'Channel of Love' and there is a tradition that anyone who manages to swim right along it will soon meet the partner of his or her dreams. Apart from its other attrac-

pp. 180-181

Sidari is set amid one of the most remarkable landscapes in Corfu, with strange rock formations creating tiny bays and narrow channels.

tions, Sidari is also a place of archaeological interest, being one of the few places on Corfu where traces of habitation in the Neolithic period have come to light. There are the ruins of a Venetian fortress nearby.

A side-road south from Sidari brings us to the village of **Arkadades**, set in bewitching

countryside where the picturesque villages are surrounded by olives and cypresses. This is, perhaps, the quietest part of Corfu, an area in which tourism has had hardly any effect on the traditional ways of life of the local people. We continue from Arkadades to the bay of **Ayios Yeorgios**, with its vast beach - 5 km. long. Although this is no longer the deserted place it once was, there is still magic in the air. The coastline north from Ayios Yeorgios is largely rocky, but there is another sandy beach at **Arillas** (2.5 km), lying between two little promontories. Three islets - Diapolo, Sykia and Gravia - are situated off the coast here.

THE SURROUNDING ISLANDS

1. THE DIAPONTIA ISLANDS: MATHRAKI - EREIKOUSA - OTHONI

To the north-west of Corfu, at distances of between 10 and 14 miles from its coast, lie a group of islands called the Diapontia which are the most westerly territory of Greece, situated where the Ionian Sea becomes the Adriatic. The largest of the islands are Mathraki, Ereikousa and Othoni, little Greek paradises where time seems to have come to a near-halt and where life flows slowly and peacefully by. All three are verdant, with olives and cypresses as the commonest trees. The very few inhabitants of the islands are fishermen, farmers and shepherds. Visitors are an even rarer sight, and this has done much to preserve the authenticity of the islands. In the summer months, caiques and launches ply to and from the islands, operating out of the harbours along the north coast of Corfu, but in the winter such sailings are few and far between and the Diapontia islands return to their isolation.

Little is known of the ancient history of the islands, and such information as we have comes from the written sources: the poet Lycophron (320-250 BC), the historian Pliny (23-79 AD), and the lexicographer Hesychius (fifth century AD). They seem to have been uninhabited in Byzantine times, and it was not until the Venetians ruled on Corfu that fresh settlers arrived, from Paxi and Epirus. During the period of the British protectorate, the Diapontia were places of exile for those who advocated the unification of the Ionian Islands with the rest of Greece. After unification actually took place in 1864, the is-

p. 183

The little islands off the coast of Corfu are just as verdant and idyllic as the 'mother island', and they complete our picture of the Ionian landscape.

Facing page: view of Paxi.

land's communities were formed into the Municipality of Diapontia, whose chief settlement is Ammos on Othoni. Today, each island is a separate administrative entity of its own, and there are some 600 permanent residents.

Mathraki

Mathraki is three nautical miles from the coast of Corfu, the closest point to it being the beach of Arillas. It has an area of 3.5 square kilometres and around 140 inhabitants, who are employed in fishing and harvesting the olives of the island. In earlier times, this was an island of sailors, owning some 30 sailing-ships, but the dwindling population brought sea-faring activities to an end. The medical and educational needs of the two villages - Ano and Kato Mathraki - are met by a rural doctor's post and by a primary school which rarely has more than seven pupils on its roll. The islanders are inter-related and take part all together in the events of community life, retaining intact all the customs and traditions of the island. They are notable for their friendly and hospitable attitude towards visitors, though tourists are few and rarely stay long, given that there is very little tourist accommodation. East of Mathraki is the uninhabited islet of Diapolo.

Ereikousa

Ereikousa is 4.5 nautical miles from Sidari, which it greatly resembles in terms of terrain. It has an area of six square kilometres and is the most populous of all the islets, with 334 permanent residents. In the centre of the island is the village of Ereikousa, around which lie the beaches of Porto, Fiki and Prangini. The islanders, hospitable and out-going, are farmers and fishermen, while the remittances of emigrants - mostly to America - make a major contribution to the island economy. Ereikousa has a hotel, and there are quite a number of rooms to rent.

Othoni

Othoni is the westernmost point in Greece, lying 7.5 miles from the north-west coast of Corfu and 43 nautical miles from Cape

p. 184
Crystal-clear water, an atmosphere of serenity, little fishing-boats: those are the charms of the Diapontia islands.

Otranto in Italy. The island has an area of nine square kilometres and two large villages, Ano and Kato Chorio (Ammos), with about 100 inhabitants. The beach near Ammos, the chief settlement, has both sand and pebbles, while there is a sandy beach at Aspri Ammos. At Aspri Ammos there is a cave which tradition claims as the home of Calypso; it would seem that in the popular mind Calypso's island, where Odysseus lived for years, was identified with Othoni. Some scholars have even gone to far as to claim that this far-flung island, and not Corfu, was Homer's Scheria, and that the palace of king Alcinous stood here. However, there is no historical evidence to back this assertion. At Kastri there are traces of a Venetian fortress, and we know that a sanatorium for British soldiers operated at Kassimatika from 1814 to 1864. During the nineteenth century, Othoni was an important trading centre, and the islanders owned about 60 sailing-ships. However, the population began to emigrate after 1850, with large numbers leaving for the United States, Australia and Germany in the 1960s. Today, such islanders as are left are farmers and fishermen, and a small proportion of their income comes from tourism. There are a few rooms to rent on Othoni, and there is also a rural doctor's post.

2. PAXI - ANTIPAXI

Paxi is the smallest of the seven major islands in the Ionian chain, with an area of 25.32 square kilometres (length 8 km., breadth 4 km.). The island lies seven nautical miles to the south of Corfu, quite close to the coast of Epirus: the channel between Paxi and Parga is only 12 nautical miles wide. There are ferry departures to Corfu town and Lefkimmi, and also to Patra, Igoumenitsa, Amfilochia and Preveza, while during the summer months launches ply back and forth to Parga. The population of Paxi is 2,400 - most of them employed in the cultivation of the olive crop and in fishing. Tourism is not particularly highly developed, and Paxi continues to be an ideal place for those who look forward to quiet holidays far from the bustle of the popular resorts.

Paxi is an island of great natural beauty; its dense covering of pines, olives and vines, its deeply indented coastline, its steep rocky cliffs and its sea-caves combine to produce a landscape of idyllic charm. The interior of the island is relatively flat - the highest 'peak', Ayios Isavros, is only 217 metres above sea level - making it ideal for walking or cycling. Walkers will find numerous paths leading down to isolated beaches. The road network is well-organised and buses run to most of the villages.

The 'capital' of Paxi, and its harbour, is **Gaios**, a quaint little town of 1,300 inhabitants whose houses are in the style typical of the Ionian islands. In the entrance to the harbour are two verdant islets, **Ayios Nikolaos** and **Panayia**, which provide natural protection against rough weather and give Gaios a magical atmosphere. On Ayios Nikolaos are the remains of a Venetian castle (1423), while on Panayia is a monastery dedicated to Our Lady. On Her feast each year (15 August), the villagers carry Her icon out into the bay on boats and there is a banquet at which all are welcome. Launches run from Gaios to these two islets, and also to Mongonisi and Kaltsonisi, two more uninhabited scraps of rock to the south of Paxi.

Further south is the second-largest village, **Ozias**, a seaside settlement of 250 inhabitants standing on a naturally amphitheatrical site. Ozias is known for its medicinal springs and for the caves to be found around its little harbour. At Porta are the remains of an Early Christian basilica. A little bridge leads across to the nearby islet of Mongonisi, which can also be reached by boat. Most of the tourist development of Paxi is centred on **Longos**, 5.5 km. north of Gaios, a typically 'Ionian' village set amid pine trees which run right down to the water's edge. On the fine beaches nearby are facilities for water-skiing, canoeing and parakiting, while fresh fish is almost always available in the little tavernas. On the north side of the island is **Lakka**, a holiday community set amid dense vegetation at the head of a bay also called Lakka. Along the coast at Lakka are numerous sea-caves, which can be visited by boat. The Ipapanti cave, according to the local people, communicates underground with the church of the Presentation of Our Lady in Lakka itself.

Antipaxi is a still tinier island, lying three nautical miles south of Paxi. It has an area of five square

kilometres and a population of about 120. There are few villages, but the island is covered with orchards, most of which belong to people from Paxi. Like Paxi, Antipaxi is densely-wooded, with clean sandy beaches and numerous caves. The nearby islets of **Exolitharo** and **Daskalio** can be visited from Antipaxi by boat. The seas around the islands are ideal for spear-fishing, and in fact most of the fish consumed on Corfu comes from Paxi and Antipaxi.

Little is known about the ancient history of these islands, and very few monuments have survived down to the present day. The written sources tell us that one of the sea-battles between the Corfiots and the pirates of Illyria took place outside the mouth of the Antipaxi channel; the Corfiot defeat in this conflict led to the surrender of the island, in 229 BC, and gave the Romans a pretext for intervening in the area (see p. 30). During the centuries which followed, the history of Paxi was largely the same as that of Corfu, and it was occupied, successively, by the Angevins, the Venetians, the French and the British. Since 1814 it has belonged administratively to the Ionian Islands, and today it is part of the Prefecture of Corfu.

p. 187

The natural environment of Paxi is of rare beauty, and the island provides visitors with an opportunity for peaceful holidays.

PRACTICAL INFORMATION

USEFUL TELEPHONE NUMBERS

(Long-distance dialling codes: 0661, 0662, 0663)

Police stations: Corfu town: 0661-39509 / Ayios Matthaios: 0661-75113 / Argyrades: 0662-51422 / Karousades: 0663-31222 / Kassiopi: 0663-81240 / Lefkimmi: 0662-22222 / Magoulades: 0663-51222 / Palaiokastritsa: 0663-41203 / Ipsos: 0661-93204 / Paxi (Gaios): 0662-32222

Tourist police: Corfu town: 0661-30265

Harbourmaster's offices: Corfu town: 0661-33096 / Palaiokastritsa: 0663-41297 / Paxi (Gaios): 0662-32259

Municipal and community offices: Corfu town: 0661-42601 / Ayios Ioannis: 0661/52208 / Ayios Matthaios: 0661-75142 / Agrafa (Sidari): -663-31100 / Alepou: 0661-31412 / Ano Korakiana: 0663-22309 / Ano Pavliana: 0661-53398 / Argyrades: 0662-51429 / Gastouri: 0661-56221 / Ereikousa: 0663-71703 / Kassiopi: 0663-81420 / Kato Korakiana: 0661-93516 / Lakones: 0663-41261 / Lefkimmi: 0662-22066 / Magoulades: 0663-51294 / Moraitika: 0661-75322 / Benitses: 0661-72284 / Nisaki: 0663-91386 / Roda: 0663-63353 / Sinarades: 0661-54014 / Paxi (Gaios): 0662-32207 (Lakka): 0662-31953

Hospitals: Corfu town: 0661/45811-5 / Lefkimmi (Health Centre): 0662-23100 / Ipsos (Health Centre): 0661-93816-8 / Paxi (Gaios Health Centre): 0662-31178

Rural doctor's posts: Ayios Matthaios: 0661-75110 / Argyrades: 0662-51422 / Avliotes (Sidari): 0663-95440 / Episkepsi: 0663-63222 / Kassiopi: 0663-81238 / Kato Garouna: 0661-53000 / Lakones: 0663-41000 / Magoulades: 0663-51050 / Moraitika (pharmacy): 0661-75330 / Benitses: 0661-72429 / Othoni: 0663-71550

OTE (telephone company) offices: Corfu town: 0661-34699 / Ayios Gordios: 0661-53207 / Ayios Matthaios: 0661-75118 / Alykes: 0661-30406 / Argyrades: 0662-51391 / Gastouri: 0661-56410 / Gouvia: 0661-91319 / Dasia: 0661-93235 / Ereikousa: 0663-71598 / Ermones: 0661-94236 / Kas-

p. 189

Corfu town from Mourayia.

siopi: 0663-81229 / Kontokali: 0661-91320 / Lefkimmi: 0662-23099 / Mathraki: 0663-71600, 95351 / Mesongi: 0661-75235 / Moraitika: 0661-71545 / Benitses: 0661-72228 / Nisaki: 0663-91214 / Othoni: 0663-71545 / Palaiokastritsa: 0663-22280 / Pelekas: 0661-94233 / Perama: 0661-39237 / Roda: 0663-63071 / Sidari: 0663-95368 / Ipsos: 0661-93234 / Paxi (Gaios): 0662-32099

Post offices: Corfu town: 0661-39604 / Lefkimmi: 0662-22355 / Paxi (Gaios): 0662-32256

New harbour: 0661-30481, 25605

Ioannis Capodistrias Airport: 0661-30180, 37398

KTEL bus station: 0661-39985

National Tourist Organisation: 0661-37638 (Casino: 0661-36540)

Museums: Archaeological Museum: 0661-30680 / Antivouniotissa Museum: 0661-38313 / Museum of Asian Art: 0661-30443 / Dionysios Solomos Museum: 0661-30674 / Museum of Banknotes (Ionian Bank): 0661-41552 / Maritime Museum: 0661-42900 / Achilleio (at Gastouri): 0661-56210 / Capodistrias Museum (at Evropouli): 0661:32440 / Historical and Folklore Museum (Sinarades): 0661-38193

Radio taxis: 0661-33811, 33813, 41333

COMMUNICATIONS

By air: There are Olympic Airways flights between **Athens** and Corfu all the year round, in approximately 50 minutes. There are also departures from Corfu for **Thessaloniki**, while charter flights link the island with **all major European destinations**. The airport is located 3 km. south of Corfu town, and transfers are carried out on Olympic Airways coaches. Information from Olympic Airways in Athens: 01-9363363 / in Corfu: 0661-38694-6 / Corfu Airport: 0661-30180, 37398.

By sea: Ferries operate all the year round from **Igoumenitsa** to Corfu town and Lefkimmi. The distance is approximately 18 nautical miles, and the trip takes 1 hour 15 minutes to Corfu town or 1 hour 30 minutes to Lefkimmi. There are also ferry sailings to **Paxi**. Information from Igoumenitsa Harbourmaster's Office: 0665-22235 / Corfu Harbourmaster's Office: 0661-33096 / Paxi Harbourmaster's Office: 0662-32259.

- There are ferry sailings from **Patra** to Corfu all the year round. Distance: 132 nautical miles, travelling time 9 hours. These ferries then sail on to **Italy (Brindisi, Bari, Ancona)**. Information from Patra Harbourmaster's Office: 061-341002 / Corfu Harbourmaster's Office: 0661-33096.

- There are ferry sailings all the year round to Corfu from **Sayiada** in **Thesprotia**; distance 13 nautical miles, sailing time 1 hour 30 minutes. Information: Sayiada Harbourmaster's Office: 0664-51217 / Corfu Harbourmaster's Office: 0661-33096.

- There are ferry sailings all the year round to Corfu from **Amfilochia** in **Aitoloakarnania** and from **Preveza** in **Epirus** (high-speed ferries, connections also to **Paxi**). The trip takes 3 hours 40 minutes. Information: Rethymniaki ticket office in Amfilochia: 0642-23162 / Preveza: 0682-32033 / Paxi: 0662-32033 / Corfu: 0661-20942-6.

- Small caiques and launches run to and from **Paxi, Mathraki, Ereikousa and Othoni**. Information: Corfu Harbourmaster's Office: 0661-33096 / Sidari Harbour Post: 0663-95330.

By road: KTEL long-distance buses operate all the year round between Corfu and Athens via Igoumenitsa. The journey takes 11 hours. Information: KTEL Athens: 01-5129443 (the bus station is at 100 Kifissou Ave.) / KTEL Corfu: 0661-39985.

- KTEL long-distance buses operate all the year round between Corfu and Thessaloniki. The journey takes 8 hours. Information: KTEL Thessaloniki: 031-528600 / KTEL Corfu: 0661-39985.

On the island: There are town bus services running out to some of the nearby villages, as follows: Afra - Ayios Ioannins - Pelekas / Kanoni - Perama - Achilleio - Gastouri - Benitses / Alykes - Kontokali - Gouvia - Kommeno - Dafnilas - Dasia / Kouramades - Vasili. Information from the bus terminus in G. Theotoki Square (Saroko), 0661-31595.

- Long-distance buses cover the routes to the more distant villages: Lefkimmi - Kavos / Korakades - Petriti / Chlomo / Stavros - Strongili / Ayios Matthaios - Vouniatades / Ano and Kato Garouna - Pentati / Sinarades - Ayios Gordios / Varypatades - Kalafationes / Glyfada - Vatos / Yannades / Ano and Kato Korakiana / Liapades - Doukades - Gardelades / Lakones - Makarades - Krini / Palaiokastritsa / Ipsos / Pyrgi / Kassiopi - Peritheia / Nymfes - Valaneio / Roda - Acharavi / Karousades / Magoulades - Velonades / Afionas - Arillas / Strinilas / Porta Sinion. Information: KTEL Corfu: 0661-39985 (Neou Frouriou Square, near the New Fortress).

- There are also taxis and firms hiring cars and motorcycles, while many of the travel agencies organise bus trips to the most popular sights.

ACCOMMODATION

Corfu has hotels, apartment complexes, rooms to rent and camp sites of all the official classes. Information: Hotel Chamber of Greece (Athens): 01-3237193 / Corfu Union of Hoteliers: 0661-22635, 52233, fax 52234 / Corfu Federation of Owners of Tourist Accommodation: 0661-26133, 23403, fax 72960, 23403.

SPORTS

- Most of the beaches on Corfu are ideal for swimming and many have facilities for water-skiing, wind-surfing and parakiting. There are diving schools at Ipsos, Palaiokastritsa and Ermones. For sailing and navigation, information from: Corfu Yacht Club: 0661-30470. There are marinas at Corfu New Harbour, on Garitsa bay (operated by the NTOG), at Gouvia, Sidari and Kassiopi. Supplies of water and fuel are available in Corfu harbour.

- For tennis, information from Corfu Tennis Club, 4 Romanou St, 0661-37021. There are also tennis courts in the hotel complexes at Alykes, Kontokali, Dafnila, Dasia, Nisaki, Roda, Ermones, Glyfada, Ayios Gordios, Moraitika and Benitses.

- In the Ropa valley, near the village of Vatos (17 km. west of Corfu town), is the golf course. Information from 27 Alexandras St in Corfu town (0661-94220), where lessons can be arranged and clubs hired. Many of the hotel complexes in Corfu town, Roda, Moraitika and Perama have mini-golf courses.

- Horse-riding facilities at Alykes and Gouvia.

- Cricket matches take place in the summer on the Spianada.

- Corfu Casino is in the Corfu Hilton International Hotel; information: 0661-36540.